The Most Beautiful Names

اسماء الحسنى

The Most Beautiful Names

Compiled by
Sheikh Tosun Bayrak al-Jerrahi al-Halveti

THRESHOLD BOOKS

This book is dedicated
to the enlightened soul of our master,
Shaikh Muhammad Muzaffereddin Ashki al-Halveti al-Jerrahi.
May his soul receive Allah's invitation:
"Oh thou soul which art at peace, return unto thy Lord,
with gladness that is thine in Him, and His in thee,
enter thou among my good servants,
enter thou my paradise."
(Surah Al-Fajr 27-30)

Threshold Books, RD 3, Box 1350, Putney, Vermont 05346

ISBN 0-939660-10-5 Paperback
ISBN 0-939669-11-3 Hardcover
Library of Congress Catalog Number: 84-50951

Printed in the United States of America

Design by Shems Friedlander

The Most Beautiful Names is another of a series of books on Sufism from the Library of the Halveti-Jerrahi Order.

The full page illustrations were photographed by Tosun Bayrak at the Grand Mosque in Bursa, Turkey.

Contents

Foreword

When we look at this world we see beauty, grandeur, sublimity, strength, the power of joy or the power of destruction manifested in it. We are attracted or repulsed by these manifestations. We feel drawn into some, absorbed or even annihilated sometimes. We feel threatened by some or inspired by awe. There is an inevitable link between what we see and feel, and ourselves.

That link is provided by the attributes of Allah. Each object manifests some power of Allah. His joy or His anger, His love or His magnificence emanates through these objects. That is why we are attracted or repelled. There is no end to these manifestations so long as the process of creation exists.

Allah's various powers are described by His Names. That is why we see that the entire creation manifests Allah's Names.

The first Man, Adam, peace be on him, was taught all the names of everything (*Qur'an* II, 31). These are the names of all objects that had come into existence by the time of his creation and all that will come into existence till Doomsday. 'Teaching the Names' means making man conscious of the essence of these things. This consciousness implies full knowledge. Full knowledge is impossible without the essence becoming part and parcel of the being. Teaching the names of things therefore implies the implanting of the essences within the being of Adam and hence the implanting of the Names of Allah in Adam's self. The attributes of Allah that were, are and are going to be manifested in this creation until Doomsday, were planted within the being of Adam. That is why Adam (peace be upon him) could represent Allah as his *Khalīfa* and become worthy of receiving the salutation of the angels. That is why Allah granted him and through him to Man the mastery of this entire creation:

It is He Who made you (His agents)
inheritors of the earth.
(*Qur'an* VI, 165)

Allah, therefore, tells us to remember Him and draw near Him by reciting His Name or His Attributes. His Name is His proper name "Allah" and His Attributes are innumerable. The Qur'an teaches us some of his Attributes. By describing the meaning and significance of those attributes which have been referred to in the Qur'an, Tosun Bayrak has satisfied a long-felt need. Though many books and philosophical treatises have been written on the Names or Attributes of Allah, there is hardly a book which sums up so succinctly the explanations that every Muslim, non-Muslim believer, and even non-believer would like to know. Who knows, this book may kindle the light of faith in many hearts. May Allah make this book a means of guiding them in the right path, Amen.

Syed Ali Ashraf
Director General
The Islamic Academy
Cambridge, 1984

أسماء الحسنى

Dedication

بسم الله الرحمن الرحيم

In the name of Allah, All-Merciful and Compassionate

Praise be to Allah, the Everlasting, and benediction to our Master Muhammad, his family, his descendants and his companions one and all.

This humble servant, full of faults, dust under the feet of the lovers of Allah, in humble compliance with the requests of my spiritual children, the light of my eye, put this composition together, after consulting the works of many saints, lovers and beloveds of Allah, who are the hand of power and the tongue of power of Allah, sanctified be their souls. For Allah says in a divine tradition about them, " . . . I become his hands . . ."

Thus ordered by my companions on the Path to Truth, I translated from the works of these masters and when it has seemed suitable a commentary has been incorporated. Let there be no doubt that this abject person and the pen in his hand is similar to "the archer and the arrow in his hand."

Should any of my spiritual brethren and the sincere seeker deign to peruse this book, I beg their forgiveness for my forgetfulness and errors, and I pray to them to remember this humble servant of Allah in their prayers of supplication. My plea to be successful is from Allah. I lean on Him and I count on Him.

بسم الله الرحمن الرحيم

BISMILLĀH AR-RAḤMĀN AR-RAḤĪM

Our beloved Prophet (Peace and Blessings of Allah be upon him) says in a hadith reported by Abu Hurayrah (May Allah be pleased with him), "There are 99 names that are Allah's alone. Whoever learns, understands and enumerates (*iḥṣa*) them enters Paradise and achieves eternal salvation."

This hadith does not mean that Allah has only 99 names. There are further names attributed to Allah in the Qur'an, and infinite others which He has revealed to His choice creation. If someone says, "So-and-so has one thousand dollars that he has reserved to give to others," does it mean that the person does not have any more money?

The ones who know say that Allah has three thousand names: one thousand He has revealed to His angels; one thousand He has revealed to His prophets; three hundred are in the *zabūr*—the psalms of David; three hundred are in the Torah; three hundred are in the Gospel; 99 are in the Holy Qur'an. One, the name of His Essence, He has kept for Himself and hidden in the Qur'an.

The beautiful names of Allah are proof of the existence and oneness of Allah. O you who are burdened and troubled with the weight and suffering of the material world, may Allah make His beautiful names a soothing balm for your wounded hearts. Learn, understand and recite Allah's beautiful names. Seek the traces of Allah's attributes in the skies above, on the earth below, and in what is beautiful in your being. You will find blessings in it to the extent of your sincerity. With the permission of Allah, the doubter will find security, the ignorant will find wisdom, the denier will confirm. The stingy will become generous, the tyrants will bow their heads, the fire in the hearts of the envious will be extinguished.

Allāh

الله

ALLĀH

Allāh is *al-ism al-a'ẓam*, the Greatest Name, which contains all the divine and beautiful attributes and is the sign of the Essence and the cause of all existence.

Allah, the cause of all existence, does not resemble in any way any of His creation. *Allāh* is Allah's name only. Nothing else can in any way assume this name nor share it. As it is said in the Qur'an, *Hal ta'lamu lahu samiyan* —"Do you know anyone who is His namesake?" (19:65).

The name *Allāh* contains five meanings, qualities that indicate the non-resemblance of Allah to anything else. They are:

Qidām He is before the before. He did not become. He always was.
Baqā' He is after the after, Eternal; He always will be.
Waḥdāniyyah He is unique, without partner, without resemblance, the cause of all. All is in need of Him, all has become by the order "Be!" and has died by His order.
Mukhalafatun lil-ḥawādith He is the Creator, bearing no resemblance to the created.
Qiyām bi-nafsihi He is self-existent, without any needs.

Allah is perfection. The extent of this perfection is infinite. The greatest name, *Allāh*, contains eight essentials indicating the perfection of Allah:

Hayyāh Allah is ever-living
'Ilm Allah is all-knowing
Sam' Allah is all-hearing
Baṣar Allah is all-seeing
Irādah All will is His

Qudrah All power is His
Takwîn All existence and actions depend upon Him
Kalām The word, all that is said and taught, is His.

The servant of Allah can relate to the divine name *Allāh*, which encompasses all names, is devoid of all faulty attributes, and contains all attributes of perfection, by seeking a wish in himself to become a perfect man. In this attempt, he could try to eliminate what is faulty in himself, and try to increase what is good in himself.

'Abdullāh is a servant who has received the highest level and honor which is possible to attain within creation, because the Creator with the secrets of all His attributes is manifested in him. Therefore, Allah Most High has called His beloved Prophet by this name. In Surah Jinn (v.19) Allah identifies His beloved, saying:

". . . the servant of Allah
stood up praying to Him."

In reality, this name belongs only to Hazrati Muhammed (Peace and Blessings of Allah be upon him) and to the *Qutubs* of any given time, who are the true inheritors of His divine wisdom, the name of Allah being the name of the Essence of Allah, the greatest name. This name is bound by the qualities of Unity and Oneness of Allah. Therefore, even if the servant has lost his proper identity in unison with Allah, his being called Abd'ullah is only metaphorical.

AR-RAḤMĀN

الرحمن جل جلاله

He is the one who wills mercy and good for all creation, at all times, without any distinction between the good and the bad, the faithful and the rebel, the beloved and the hated. He pours upon all creation infinite bounties. The proof is in the Qur'an: *wa raḥmatī wasi'at kulla shay'īan*-"My Mercy covers everything" (7:156)

The ones who know have interpreted the meaning of *Raḥmān* as the will of the total good of Allah, *irādat al-khayr*, and say that *Raḥmān*, like *Allāh*, is a proper name of the Creator, and cannot be attributed to others. The meaning of this mercy is a fineness of feeling, a pain and concern felt when one knows that someone is in distress. It begins with this pain, whose pressure moves us to help the one in distress. But the feeling of mercy and pity is not sufficient. Real compassion is in force when one is able to alleviate the pain and distress which the pitied one is suffering. Allah is beyond of all these, yet He opted for compassion rather than punishment before He created creation. He has created all creation with His mercy. Everything which has come to be since the beginning is blessed with mercy. He has created all creation, including His supreme creation, man, without defect and pure. He has blessed His creation with infinite bounty. In His mercy, He has shown the dangers of loss and perdition. He has given man and only man the freedom of choice between good and bad.

Find in yourself the light of *Raḥmān* by using your freedom of choice for the good of yourself and of others. Feel the pain of the misguided one as well as the unfortunate one, not with condemnation, but with pity and assistance.

Abu Hurayrah (May Allah be pleased with him) reports the Messenger of Allah (Peace and Blessings of Allah be upon him) as saying, "Allah Most High has one hundred portions of mercy. He has sent only one portion upon the universe and divided it among all His creation. The feeling of mercy and compassion that His creatures feel among themselves is out of that share. The other 99 portions He has saved for the Day of Last Judgment when He will bestow them upon the believers."

Another hadith reflecting the will and wish of Allah to offer His compassion and beneficence to the creation is: "If one does not need and ask Allah [for His compassion and beneficence], Allah will direct His anger towards him."

'Abd ar-Raḥmān is he in whom Allah expresses His mercy upon the universe. Every son and daughter of Hz. Adam (May Allah bless him) takes their share of the mercy from the Merciful in accordance with their potential. None are excluded from this expression of the Merciful, as the Prophet (Peace and Blessings of Allah be upon him), Allah's mercy upon the universe, says in a tradition:

"Allah has created man in the form of his mercy."

AR-RAḤĪM

الرحيم جل جلاله

He is the source of infinite mercy and beneficence, who rewards with eternal gifts the ones who use His bounties and beneficence for the good. This is mentioned in the Qur'an: *wa kāna bil-mu'minīna Raḥīman*—"He is compassionate and beneficent [only] to the believers" (33:43).

Ar-Raḥīm indicates beneficence toward those who have a will and choice, and who use it according to Allah's will and for His pleasure. When Allah says, "I have created all for you . . ." that is the expression of His *raḥmāniyyah*. When we find this bounty hidden in everything, including ourselves, and use it as He wills us, caring for it as it is left to us to do for His sake, we are rewarded with eternal salvation. Allah says, " . . . and I created you for Myself." This great honor is the expression of His *raḥīmiyyah*.

Hz. Mujāhid (May Allah be pleased with him) said, "*Raḥmān* belongs to the people of this world; *Raḥīm* belongs to those of the Hereafter." The ones who know pray: *yā Raḥmān ad-dunyā wa Raḥīm al-ākhirah*—"O *Raḥmān* of the world and *Raḥīm* of the Hereafter." *Raḥmān* is mercy upon the *nafs*, the worldly being. *Raḥīm* is mercy upon the heart. *Raḥmān* gives sustenance in this world. *Raḥīm* gives eternal salvation in the Hereafter.

The manifestation of *raḥīmiyyah* in the believers occurs as thankfulness to Allah, who gives all, and also as the ability to be compassionate, caring and giving, which He also gives us. Absence of pride in being instrumental in doing good deeds, and realization that He is the Creator of the ones in need as well as the satisfaction of their needs, in extending Allah's beneficence upon those who need it—all this reflects *raḥmāniyyah*.

If you should encounter difficulties, unthankfulness and resentment, you should bear it for Allah's sake, because you will receive your reward here and tenfold in the Hereafter. Do not show off your good deeds, especially to their recipients. Be thankful to them; if their conditions did not exist, your compassion and generosity could not be exercised.

As for the recipients of compassion and care, they should be thankful to their benefactors and remember them well at all times, because "The one who cannot be thankful to man cannot be thankful to Allah." But they should not make gods out of their benefactors, becoming their servants instead of Allah's servants. They should know that good comes only from Allah; but the tool that He has chosen is a beautiful tool, worthy of respect.

The ones who find the taste of Allah's attributes of *Raḥmān* and *Raḥīm* in their beings, and come close to their Creator through them, cannot have doubt and sadness in their hearts. They know that whatever happens, Allah, ar-Rahman, ar-Rahim, will have mercy upon them, save them, and reward them.

On the other hand, the ones who think that Allah's compassion, mercy and beneficence which appear in them are their own qualities, becoming arrogant, are bound to become of the doubters. That doubt, in extreme cases, may push man to take his own life.

'Abd ar-Raḥīm is the pious one whose fear and love of Allah are constant. His life is a constant effort to perfect himself in accordance with the prescriptions of Islam, and he is the one with whom Allah is pleased. He is the one who is honored with the manifestation of Allah's compassion and beneficence, which he expresses towards other believers.

AL-MALĪK

الملك جل جلاله

He is the Owner of the universe, of the whole creation—the absolute Ruler. Allah is the only Ruler of the entire universe, visible and invisible, and of all creation, from before the beginning and after the end. There is none like Him because He is the Creator of His kingdom, which He created from nothing. Only He knows the size of His kingdom, the number of its population, and the strength of His armies. Only His will, His rule and His justice exist. What happens is what He wills; what He does not will will never happen. He does not need His kingdom, His kingdom needs Him. He rules by Himself; He does not need any means of help to rule. He has created the universe as a place of work for His creation, and has created the Day of Last Judgment as a great court of justice. In the world, one's deeds are planted. On the Day of Last Judgment the rewards are reaped. Everyone will receive the result of his doings. There is none other than Him in whom to take refuge.

Servants of Allah who come to know their Master, finding the meaning of that divine name in themselves, will become sober from the drunkenness of counting their fortunes, their high positions and their fame as their own. Those who have served worldly kings as gods will wish for the Master of their masters. All will know that they are not left on their own in this divine kingdom, but that there is an absolute Ruler who sees a black ant crawling on a black rock on the darkest of nights, as well as the most secret thoughts and feelings passing through minds and hearts. Everything that one is and everything that one does is watched and recorded; all will be accounted for on the Day of Last Judgment.

One who knows *al-Malīk*, even if he is a king, will know that at best he is a shepherd charged for a short time to care for a flock that is not his. To the extent of his conscientiousness, hard work and devotion, he may expect to be rewarded by his master. If he is a bad shepherd, killing and roasting the lambs, drinking all their milk, letting the wolves ravage the flock, he certainly will be punished. When his duty as a shepherd ends, he will have to give an accounting. It is better to put one's accounts in order before the day that they must be submitted.

'Abd al-Malīk is the servant who has been given the power and control over his own life and actions, as well as the life of others, to the extent of the orders and will of Allah. The manifestation of the name *yā Malīk*, the abolute King of the universe, upon a servant of Allah is the hardest to bear and the most powerful of the attributes manifested in man.

AL-QUDDŪS

القدوس جل جلاله

He is the most pure one, devoid of all blemish, shortcoming, weakness, heedlessness and error.

Al-Quddūs is the equivalent of the attribute *mukhālafatun lil-ḥawādith*—He is the Creator "bearing no resemblance to the created." This is one of the five qualities that indicate the non-resemblance of Allah to anything.

Al-Quddūs is the unique purity that is Allah's, whereby His essence, His attributes, His names, His words, His actions, His justice, are devoid of all blemish. He bears no resemblance, in any of His attributes or actions, to even the most perfect of His creatures. Even the most perfect creatures have something lacking in their essence, attributes, actions, judgments, or words. For one thing, they are temporal, while Allah—the most perfect, the most pure, is eternal, free of time and place. Before existence there was no time and no place, but Allah existed.

The believers who understand and feel this divine purity will wish to praise Allah for His perfection (*taqdīs*) and will remember to avoid attributing any qualities that are defective or any temporal imperfect state to Allah (*tasbīḥ*).

To find the feeling of *al-Quddūs* in oneself, one should work on cleansing one's faith by eliminating doubts. Faith is a whole. The existence of a single doubt blemishes it. One should try to cleanse one's devotions and prayers by sincerity. Sincerity in prayer is to pray to Allah for Allah's sake, for no other purpose, seeking no other benefit. Otherwise the prayer itself becomes *shirk*, the unforgivable sin of associating equals with Allah. One should try to cleanse one's heart by abandoning bad habits; bad habits are like garbage and thorns, and our hearts are Allah's houses. He says, "I do not fit in heavens and earth, but I fit into the hearts of My believing servants."

'Abd al-Quddūs is he whose heart is cleansed and purified, and contains none but Allah. A heart filled with Allah is safe from all but Him entering it. The manifestation of the name *Yā Quddūs*, the Most Pure, could only appear in a heart described by Allah in the Holy Tradition: "I do not fit into the heavens and the earth, but I fit within the heart of my faithful servant."

AS-SALĀM

السلام جل جلاله

In the Qur'an Allah says, *salāmun kawlan min rabbin raḥīm*—the Beneficent Lord sends a *salām*—peace, blessing, protection, salvation, and salutation—to the believers in Paradise (36:57). In this ayat Allah al-Rahim rewards the believers with the security and joy of the wished-for Paradise. He is the one who saves the believing servants from all dangers, bringing them the peace, blessing, and security of Paradise. *As-Salām* is this state of being free of all fault, error, danger and trouble. In this it resembles the divine name *al-Quddūs*, but it pertains to the future. It also means the one who is persisting, uninterrupted, unfaltering, unweakening, continuing to eternity.

Those who find the peace and security of *as-Salām* in their hearts believe in and depend on Allah in all their affairs, and know that by the grace of that name they will be saved from all dangers and difficulties. When they are saved from a danger by someone, they see the real savior, although they are also thankful to the intermediary. A Turkish proverb says, "Don't lean on a tree that will but dry up and decay; don't depend on men, they will but age and die." The one who depends on Allah, *as-Salām*, the savior, will never panic. Allah's strength will show itself in him as the fearlessness of the believer. This is the manifestation of *as-Salām*.

Patience is also a manifestation of *as-Salām*. Allah says, "If

I give a pain to my servant either through his body or possessions or his family or children and he encounters this with the strength of patience and belief in Me, I would be embarrassed to weigh his deeds and to look into the books of his actions on the Day of Last Judgment."

'Abd as-Salām is the one whom Allah protects against all trouble, need, and shame.

AL-MU'MIN

المؤمن جل جلاله

He is the Illuminator of the light of faith in hearts.

He is the Comforter, the Protector of the ones who take refuge in Him. Faith is the security that protects one from all dangers; therefore it is the greatest gift of Allah. The absence of fear in the heart of the believer is commensurate with the degree of his faith.

Men have enemies who continuously try to harm them, to disturb their peace, to lead them astray. The worst of those enemies are their own egos and the accursed Devil. The tyrants, the maligners, the enviers, come after them. When one says "I take refuge in Allah," one takes refuge in the attribute of *al-Mu'min*. He does not refuse anyone who takes refuge in Him. But to have faith in *al-Mu'min*, one has to have faith first. In Islam there are three degrees of faith.

1. Confirmation of one's faith by one's words so that others hear that you believe in Allah, in His Prophet (Peace and Blessings of Allah be upon him) and in the truth of all that he says and does.

2. Confirmation by one's acts; doing what is lawful, and abstaining from what is unlawful.

3. Confirmation by the heart; the firm belief, without any conditions or doubts, in the truth of the Prophet's (Peace and Blessings of Allah be upon him) traditions.

What is essential is faith in the heart. If that leaves, may

Allah protect us, one becomes of the non-believers. The one who confirms his faith with his words while his heart is not with Allah is a liar. The one who goes as far as acting as if he believed is a hypocrite. If he is a believer at heart, and for some reason cannot declare it or cannot act upon his faith, he is still a believer.

Watch your faith and your actions as a believer. This is the reflection of *al-Mu'min*. Be the dependable one in whom others find security. Be the one who does not deny help to those who take refuge in Him, and you will have a taste of *al-Mu'min*, the Most Secure.

'Abd al-Mu'min is he who has been given refuge by Allah from all disasters, pain and punishment. The property, honor and life of others is safe with and saved by the servant in whom the name *al-Mu'min* is manifested.

AL-MUHAYMIN

He is the Protector and the Guardian. He is the one who sees to the evolution and the growth of His creation, leading them where they are destined to go. Nothing escapes His attention for a moment. He is the one who watches the good deeds and rewards them fully. He counts the sins exactly, not adding to their punishment even an amount the size of a mustard seed.

One may find the reflection of *al-Muhaymin* in oneself through consciousness and awareness—by watching intently one's actions, words, thoughts and feelings, and by trying to control them.

'Abd al-Muhaymin is he who sees the existence and the rules of Allah in everything. In expression of the name *yā Muhaymin* he watches over himself and others, guarding against wrong and helping them to secure the things to which they have a right.

Allāh Al-Mu'min, Al-Muhaymin, Al-'Azīz, Al-Jabbār, Al-Mutakabbir

العزيز جل جلاله ١٤

AL-'AZĪZ

He is the Victorious One whom no force can overwhelm.

There is no strength in this universe that can stand before this will. *Al-'Azīz* appears often in the Holy Qur'an in relation to verses of punishment. Although Allah's power is victorious over all, like the true victor, He delays punishment. He does not hurry to destroy the one who persists in revolt and sin.

The one who is strong, but does not exercise his strength, who is not vengeful, reflects the beautiful name of *al-'Azīz*. One may find the traces of *al-'Azīz* in oneself if one is able to suppress the demands of one's ego and flesh. Also, one should seek to satisfy one's lawful needs through clean, honest, lawful means. If one stays within the limits of wisdom and clearsightedness in all one's thoughts and actions, one may see one's portion of Allah's attribute of *al-'Azīz*.

'Abd al-'Azīz is he whom Allah has rendered safe from all attacks and powers while granting him victory over all powers which oppose him.

الجبار جل جلاله

AL-JABBĀR

He is the Repairer of the broken, the Completer of the lacking, the one who can enforce His will without any opposition.

Hz. 'Ali (May Allah be pleased with him) used to pray, *Yā Jābbira kulli kasīrin wa yā musahilla kulli 'asīrin*—"O *Jabbār*, the one who puts together all that is broken and the one who brings ease to every difficulty."

At the same time He is the one who is able to enforce His

will at all times and places without any opposition. This forcefulness makes submission a necessity. His forcefulness is within the destiny of all His creation. The sun cannot say, "I will not rise again." The wind cannot say, "I will not blow again." Yet man is given the choice. He is also given the wisdom to know what is right and what is wrong. He is given freedom; yet the purpose of his creation is to know Allah, to find Allah and to become the servant of Allah. But this is not enforced on him. Allah has left it to his wish.

One finds *al-Jabbār* by knowing that the only place to go to repair one's broken hopes, to find peace in the confusion in which one finds oneself, is to Allah. On these unhappy occasions of disobedience and revolt, if one runs to take refuge in Allah's mercy before the coming of Allah's punishment (from which no force can save one and from which there is nowhere to hide), one will find in this feeling the reflection of Allah the Forceful One.

'Abd al-Jabbār is the one who reflects Allah's force, who dominates everything and enforces Allah's will in the material and spiritual creations.

AL-MUTAKABBIR

المتكبر جل جلاله

He is the Greatest, who shows His greatness in everything, on all occasions. The manifestation of greatness belongs only to Allah. The creation, whose being or not being depends on the will and the single order of Allah, does not have the right to assume this name.

Of all the creation, the first one who became arrogant and claimed greatness was the accursed Devil. Then there are those who have followed the Devil, who think that the power, intelligence, knowledge, position, fame, and fortune that Allah has lent to them momentarily are theirs, so that they become proud.

If man thought of his beginning and his end, which are very close to each other, he would remember that his "before" was a drop of sperm transplanted from his father's urinary tract to his mother. His end will be to become a limp, cold, yellow corpse that cannot be borne even by the ones who loved him and that will be thrown into a hole in the ground.

Where are the Pharoahs, the Nimrods, Napoleons and Hitlers?

Al-Mutakabbir is an honor fit only for Allah. The created one cannot assume this attribute. Allah al-Mutakabbir is the adversary of the proud man. He will humiliate him, making him the lowest of the low. Just as the rain that comes from the skies does not gather on the tops of high mountains, Allah's blessings and compassion gather in lowly places.

The ones who wish to feel the divine attribute of *al-Mutakabbir* will find it only when they work hard to try to achieve the highest level of their potential, while never boasting of or even revealing their greatness.

'Abd al-Mutakabbir is he who is shown his smallness and the greatness of Allah. His egotism and pride are effaced and replaced by the greatness of Allah reflected in him. He is safe from being belittled and bows to none other than the Truth.

AL-KHĀLIQ

الخَالِقُ جلّ جلاله

He is the one who creates from nothing, creating at the same time the states, conditions, and sustenance of all that He has created. He establishes how, when, and where creation will take place. He creates in accordance with this order. Everything from the beginning to the end of the created existences has been established in goodness and wisdom. In accordance with the perfect order, everything follows the path it will follow. There are no accidents in the universe.

Allah al-Khaliq did not need the creation, nor does He receive any benefit from it. Perchance the reason for creation is that He may acknowledge His eternal will of greatness and power, and see His own beauty and perfection. For He says, "I was a hidden treasure. I loved to be known, so I created creation."

Allah existed. None existed with Him, yet there was nothing lacking or missing before He created the creation. When He created the universe, nothing was added, nor was anything diminished.

Man, the supreme creation, should know that "Allah has created all for man and man for Himself." All creation, and the order that it follows, is total beneficence and wisdom. One must find these benefits and this wisdom, use them, and feel the blessing of being a part of this creation which is a reflection of the Creator.

'Abd al-Khāliq is the one whom Allah has rendered able to do all in accordance with Allah's will.

AL-BĀRI' البارئ جل جلاله

He is the one who orders His creation with perfect harmony—not only each thing harmonious within itself, but everything in accordance with everything else. This infinite-seeming universe works like a clock. All is for one and one is for all. See how everything in you is connected, working together, and how, when a part fails, all else is affected.

The functions of one and all depend upon each other. Try

to see to it that this harmony that is in your nature is manifested in your life. Allah al-Bari' gave you intelligence to help you to know your Creator. He also gave you freedom of will and choice so that you may choose the right over the wrong. But if you use your will to opt for the wrong, and your mind to deny the existence of the Creator, then you will be attempting to destroy the universal harmony; you will end up destroying yourself.

'Abd al-Bāri' is the one who is saved from incongruity, error, injustice and confusion. He is made to act in perfect order, regularity and uniformity with the divine laws working in nature; he is also able to help and inspire others to do so. The attribute of *yā Bāri'*, the one who renders harmony, is actually part of Allah's attribute *ar-Raḥmān*, the Beneficent. As it is mentioned in Surah Rahman; "Thou seest no incongruity in the Creation of the Beneficent. Then look again, can thou see any disorder." Therefore, *'Abd al-Bāri'* is beneficient in his harmoniousness.

AL-MUṢAWWIR

The perfect artist who gives everything the most unique and beautiful form is *al-Muṣawwir*. He is the one who, without using any model, shapes everything in the most perfect shape. No two things are the same—look at your fingerprints. Each and every creation is a choice creation, an expression of Allah's infinite beneficence and wisdom.

These three beautiful names of Allah—The Creator, the Maker of Perfect Harmony, the Shaper of Unique Beauty—are the attributes of Allah that are manifested in the nearest and liveliest way in man. Man makes, builds, shapes many beautiful and useful things manifesting these attributes in himself—but he misjudges.

The artist says that he "creates" beauty. The engineer "invents" a flying machine. They think that it is they who do this. They even forget the other men who might claim that they "created" the paint and the brush, and the sciences of geometry, physics, and mathematics, without whose "creation" their "creation" could not have been possible. They forget about the sources that produced the materials for that "creation."

Who created the mind, the eyes, and the hands that put all this together? That which man makes depends on many conditions, materials and helpers. Allah's creative act does not depend on any model, material, time, tool, helper, or anything else. When He creates, He says *Kun*, "Be!" and a whole universe becomes. Allah's treasure is between two letters, "K" and "N"—or between "B" and "E." What man must do, instead of claiming to be a "creator," is to try to see the divine power of creativity. He should try to lead others who seek to find Allah al-Khaliq, al-Bari', al-Musawwir, and help them to find Him through His creative manifestations.

'Abd al-Muṣawwir is the maker of things in accordance with the beauty, manifest in all that Allah has created, because no beauty is possible in opposition to the beauty created by Allah or other than it.

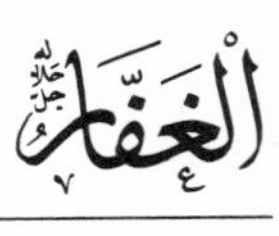

AL-GHAFFĀR

He is the one who accepts repentance and forgives. If one is guilty of the disruption of harmony within oneself and around oneself, which is perhaps the greatest sin, and one realizes, wills and begs Allah's help not to do it again, if one begs with tears of shame and asks Allah al-Ghaffar for forgiveness, Allah will forgive one and perhaps transform one's sin into a good deed.

A sinner is like a poor fellow who has fallen into a sewer. What is the first thing that he must do? He cannot face others in that state, nor can he stand himself. He must wash and cleanse himself, unless he is insane, not realizing his offensive state. The soap and water with which to wash one's interior is repentance. Woe to those who do not see nor smell the dirty stench filling their interiors!

Repentance is between each person and Allah; no one else need hear it. It need not even be pronounced. Allah knows what passes through one's heart. Repentance must also be accompanied by a firm intention not to do the sinful act again. The sign of acceptance of your repentance and the accordance of forgiveness by Allah al-Ghaffar, is that He will not let you repeat that sinful act again.

'Abd al-Ghaffār is the one who is given the quality of forgiving a fault, of covering and hiding a fault from others, of having the compassion of not seeing a fault as a fault. He does this in cases and to persons whom Allah, the Forgiver, has forgiven.

AL-QAHHĀR

القهّار جلّ جلاله

He is the Ever-Dominating One, who has surrounded all His creation from without and within with His irresistible power. Nothing can escape Him. The worlds and the heavens bow their heads before of Him. How many universes, races, and nations has He destroyed in punishment!

Allah counters His attribute of *al-Qahhār* with His attribute *al-Laṭīf*. They are within each other. He has also created causes and means that separate His punishing destructive force from His delicate loving finesse (*al-Laṭīf*). He has created the means of faith, sincerity, justice, compassion, generosity, wisdom, and other beautiful characteristics upon

Allāh Al-Ghaffār, Al-Qahhār, Al-Wahhāb

which the light of *al-Laṭīf* shines. He has created the causes of rebellion, denial, arrogance, ignorance, tyranny and hypocrisy, upon which the darkness of His terror is reflected.

Try to find the traces of these ascending and descending causes, and these two mirrors—one full of light, the other, darkness—in and around you. We take refuge from Allah al-Qahhar in Allah al-Latif.

'Abd al-Qahhār is the one who is given the power to obliterate tyranny. None can influence him nor can overcome him. He becomes all-powerful to execute that which is right.

AL-WAHHĀB الوهّاب جلّ جلاله

He is the donor of all, without conditions, without limits, without asking any benefit or return, giving everything to everyone, everywhere, always. He gives money to the poor, health to the sick, children to those who are barren, freedom to the trapped, knowledge to the ignorant.

From the smallest necessity to the greatest fortune, He is the creator of everything—of the one who is in need, his needs, and the satisfaction of his needs. If *al-Wahhāb* were not such a giver, no one would receive anything, ever.

When *al-Wahhāb* gives to you, no one can prevent that good from coming to you. And when He gives to someone else, no force in the world could divert that good to you.

Allah has created a creation of donors who give without expecting return. But because they are not the creators of the things given through their hands, they are but signs of Allah's attribute of *al-Wahhāb*. A man, like a tree, can give only so much to so few, for a limited time only. The ones who receive from them love them and are thankful to them. How much thanks, then, is due to the one who gives infinitely to all His creation?

A man gives, but is in need of a response, at least of recognition or thankfulness from the recipient. Above all, he needs to receive the thing in order to give it. A tree which gives fruit, a goat which gives milk, need care, water, food.

Allah needs nothing, so His is the true gift.

'Abd al-Wahhāb is he through whom Allah gives whatever He wishes. He becomes the donor of infinite gifts, without expecting any return, for no particular purpose, to those who are in need and who are worthy.

AR-RAZZĀQ

الرزاق جل جلاله

He is the Sustainer. Sustenance is needed to maintain the creation. There is a physical sustenance and a spiritual sustenance. In the case of man, one should count as physical sustenance not only food, drink, air and clothing but also one's mother and father, husband or wife and children as well. Even one's possessions and knowledge are part of one's sustenance.

All that is included in what we call natural laws is also included in material sustenance. There is nothing empty or useless in the universe. Every single creation is a treasure, as is indicated in the ayat *Rabbanā mā khalaqta hādha bāṭilan*—"Our Lord, You have not created this universe in vain" (3:190). All material sustenance is pure in origin. Only if it is soiled by the hand of man does it become undesirable, hateful and unlawful. Therefore man first has to seek and find the elements of sustenance in everything. The one who cannot receive his sustenance because he does not make any effort is of the unsustained, which is a curse. And again, if man soils by his dirty hands the pure sustenance given to him, he is of those who partake of what is unlawful.

The spiritual sustenances are contained in the holy books,

but some holy books, although originally pure, have also been soiled by the hand of man. Not so the Holy Qur'an, the last and final sacred book, which has not been tampered with. Not even a dot has been changed. Just as one has to make efforts to gain material sustenance, one will receive one's spiritual sustenance from the Holy Qur'an to a degree equal to the extent of one's efforts.

'Abd ar-Razzāq is he whom Allah has rendered rich. He becomes a source for others to gain their sustenance with ease and in abundance.

AL-FATTĀḤ الفتّاح جلّ جلاله

He is the Opener and the Solver, the Easer of all that is locked, tied and hardened. There are things that are closed to one. There are states and problems that are tied in a knot. There are hardened things that one cannot see through and pass through. Some are material things: professions, jobs, gains, possessions, places, friends that are unavailable to one. There are also hearts tied in a knot with sadness, minds tied up in doubts or questions they are unable to answer.

Allah al-Fattah opens them all. There is nothing unavailable to the beloved servant of Allah, for whom *al-Fattāḥ* opens all gates. No force can keep those doors locked. But if Allah does not open the doors of His blessings, no force can make those doors open. He has the key to the treasure of sacred secrets that is the heart of man, Allah's very own house.

Stand at the gate of Allah's mercy, and knock on the door of *al-Fattāḥ*. He certainly will open it sooner or later. Pray and want things from Allah unceasingly, always. You are poor, He is Rich. You are in need, He is the Satisfier of needs. You are in the dark, He is the Light. If Allah wills you will see *al-Wahhāb* when he opens the door.

You yourself, open your doors of mercy and generosity; help those who are weaker than you so that you will be saved from the tyranny of those who are stronger than you. Help the ones who are fallen, so that you will be helped when you fall. Above all, do not hurt anyone, because that is the key which locks the doors of mercy and blessings.

'Abd al-Fattāḥ is the one who has been given the key to the secrets of all knowledge. He opens knots believed to be fast, secrets which are hidden, hearts which are tight, bounties which are reserved.

AL-'ALĪM

العليم جل جلاله

He is the one who knows all. He knows what has happened, what is happening, and what will happen from the beginning to the end. All existence is present at all times in the knowledge of *al-'Alīm*. Nothing can be left out, no one can hide himself. All existence exists by His creation, within the limitations of the conditions He has created; it knows as much as Allah has permitted it to know. Yet there is no limit to Allah's knowledge.

In comparison to what one knows of this creation, what one does not know is infinite. This world of ours is like our very own house. For these millions of years we have inhabited it, yet we still do not know what is hidden in the closets, in the attic and in the basement. Sometimes we are like someone who is dying of hunger who has a treasure buried a foot under him. Our knowledge stays on the surface of a very few things. When we attempt to look under the surface, we see our impotence.

And what about the future? We do not know what is going

to happen to us the next moment. What is this human life in comparison to the infinite past and the infinite future? It is a blink of the eye. How much can one see? Happy is he who can see that he cannot see.

Indeed Allah bestows upon you all sorts of blessings, perfections comensurate to you. He taught you His names, and what is right and what is wrong. But your life is limited. Your power is limited. Your knowledge is limited. You are limited. Try to feel the unlimited perfection, the unlimited knowledge of Allah, Knower of all, and seek His pleasure. Eternal salvation is contained within all that.

'Abd al-'Alīm is he who is given wisdom without learning anything from anyone, without studying or thinking, only due to the purity and the light with which he was created. The knowledge which *'Abd al-'Alīm* receives is called *'irfān*, which is to know the Truth as the Truth.

AL-QĀBIḌ, AL-BĀSIṬ القابض الباسط

He is the one who constricts, and He is the one who releases. All existence is in the palm of Allah's Hand of Power. He may close His hand and prevent wealth, happiness, family, children and comfort from coming to one. The rich turn poor, the healthy become sick, the happy become sad. The comfortable heart becomes constricted, the clear mind becomes depressed. These are manifestations of Allah's attribute *al-Qābiḍ*.

Then He opens His hand and releases abundance, joy, relief, and ease. These are manifestations of His attribute *al-Bāsiṭ*.

Allah knows all. He is the All-Merciful, He is the Judge, He is the one who guides the life of His creation. His is the will. The life on this planet is a test for us, but Allah does test His servants above their ability. He tries us with trials that He knows we can pass.

At the times of constriction, your *nafs* and your flesh will suffer, but your essence should balance that state with patience *(ṣabr)*, which is the companion of faith. "Allah loves those who are patient." Profit from the times of constriction *(qabḍ)*, which may be means of strengthening your faith, bringing you closer to your Creator, making you His beloved.

Do not be spoiled by the periods of comfort and ease (*basṭ*), when all is going well, forgetting Allah in your excitement and pleasure, and becoming arrogant, thinking that you are the cause of your success and your security. These are the times to remember the other companion of faith, thankfulness (*shukr*).

Adab, right behavior, is the means by which one can encounter and solve the problems which may arise in the states of constriction (*qabḍ*) and ease (*basṭ*). This will prevent one from going into a state of disorientation, confusion and doubt at times of depression, *qabḍ*, and overexuberance at times of ease, *basṭ*.

Keep a balanced state with the knowledge that "all good and bad comes from Allah," and that a fine wisdom, unknown to us, is in Allah's judgment. Whatever happens, tie your heart to Allah's prescriptions and Allah's pleasure, and continue doing your duties as Allah's good servant.

Such faithful ones, well balanced and serious, will certainly gain Allah's help, approval, and love.

'Abd al-Qābiḍ is he who closes his own being to prevent unworthy influences from entering and helps others to do the same. At the same time, he knows that it is not right to hold too tight to one's own and others' egos, as Allah is the Best Judge and knows best. If one held the control of one's ego too tight, it would be like trying to control one's destiny. *'Abd al Quābiḍ* holds with the hand of Allah and as tight as Allah, *al-Qābīd, wills.*

ʿAbd al-Basit gives freely of his efforts, and from what he possesses in accordance with Allah's will, to bring joy to the hearts of Allah's servants. He is generous on the exterior and generous in his inner being. In him, the secret of al-Batin, the Inner Existence, is also manifested. He brings that which is inner in him and in others to the surface, but in this and in other actions, he does nothing which is contrary to the *shariah*, Allah's prescriptions.

AL-KHĀFIḌ, AR-RĀFIʿ الخافض جل جلاله الرافع جل جلاله

He is the Abaser and the Exalter.

Allah Most High is the one who raises His creatures to honor and fame and who can cast them down to be the lowest of the low. Often this action of the Creator is manifested in the states of those who do not recognize Allah, refuse to obey His rules, and exalt themselves in arrogance, becoming tyrants who dismiss the rights of others. The one abased by Allah can only be raised by Him.

Allah is merciful. Such treatment may shake the heedless out of their sleep. Then, although painful, the state of abasement at the hand of *al-Khāfiḍ* becomes a great gift for the one who wakes up and sees the hand that raises and the hand that lowers.

Know that although it is Allah who exalts and abases, the cause is always you. In His mercy, He delays His harsh lessons so that you may realize yourself and change your ways. Do not feel secure, for your state, your actions both material and spiritual, unmistakeably will always result in the terrible abasement or the rewarding exaltation.

Allah exalts those who have the conduct of angels, who have sweet tongues, who prefer to give rather than receive, who hide the faults of others instead of criticizing, who build instead of destroying, who are strong yet gentle. He exalts them, enlightening their hearts with faith, knowledge and truth, and makes His creatures love and respect them. As long as they persist in their enlightened way, Allah further heightens their state.

But those who refuse to acknowledge the purpose of their creation, letting their egos ride them and lead them astray into lies and cheating, setting traps for each other, fighting each other shamelessly—these are the unfaithful ones who are like animals dressed up in the fine clothes of kings. They make a lot of noise and raise a lot of dust; in that they attract attention, but they are no more than dogs fighting for a bone.

Allah the Abaser strips them of their fine clothes and shows their real shape. It is hoped they will learn; it is hoped they will serve as lessons to others.

'Abd al-Khāfiḍ protects himself and others from abasement. The protection of Allah's servant from influences which cause degradation is an opportunity to see the Truth.

'Abd ar-Rāfi' sees the magnificence of the Creator in the created, including in himself, and with this rising into high levels of consciousness, comes closer to Allah. He is exalted, and in turn he exalts others who are worthy. He who tries to rise does so because he wishes and begs to reach Allah's Beneficience. Often he in whom the name ar-Rafi', the Exalter, is manifest, also receives the expression of Allah's attribute of ar-Rahim, the Beneficent; beneficence comes through him to all around him.

AL-MU'IZZ, AL-MUDHILL المعز المذل

He is the one who honors and the one who humiliates.

In honor and humiliation there is the implication of raising and lowering. The one who has honor has received a state of pride and dignity (*'izzah*). But this state of pride and dignity obtained from Allah, the One who Honors, is very different from the pride that man imagines he deserves (*kibr*). The pride and dignity of the one who is honored by Allah is not pride in himself, but respect paid to the honor given him, and to the One who gives honor.

Indeed, he is still a human being. He needs to eat and drink—and he does that lawfully, and in good measure. For Allah, as part of the honor He has bestowed upon him, has given him the wisdom and joy of obtaining the necessities and enjoyments of this world with His good pleasure. Such a servant of Allah will not stray from Allah's permission and pleasure even if it means death for him, because within the gift of the Honorer to the honored is a safeguard against the disgrace of the divine gift.

However, the honor that one attributes to oneself or that is attributed to one by other creatures of Allah is a curse that distorts one's reality, making one imagine that one is in a state other than one's own. Knowledge of oneself leads one to one's Lord. But imagining oneself to be other than one's real self leads one to the Devil. His feature is arrogance, the cause of his expulsion from Allah's presence. That was the first act of Allah in His manifestation of the Humiliator.

Then there are those who have neither the dignity and honor awarded by Allah nor false pride that they make up themselves, but who are undignified, shameless and disgraceful. Their hearts are on fire with the ambition of this world. No good comes from them to anything or anyone because they are selfish and stingy. There is no limit to the degree to which they will humble themselves to beg for the goods of this world. They are guilty of *shirk*, attributing equals to Allah, because they take those temporal hands that throw bones to them as their gods.

The one who asks and hopes from Allah alone knows that all honor is His and can come only from Him. Those who think they are the fashioners of their own destinies and can get what they want by themselves, who seek the praise of creatures and are arrogant—these are the followers of the Devil. They will receive the punishment of the Devil, and will be expelled from the presence and the care of Allah.

The ones who lower themselves and worship creatures, hoping to receive good from them, will be further humiliated by Allah, and tyrannized by those creatures whom they take for their temporal gods.

'Abd al-Mu'izz is honored with the friendship of Allah, thus rising to the highest summit of honor and fortune, and appearing so to the whole creation.

'Abd al-Mudhill is he who is made an example of degradation. Often Allah manifests His attribute of abaser in His enemies.

AS-SAMĪ' السميع جل جلاله

He is the one who hears all—that which comes from the lips, passes through the minds, is felt by the hearts; the rustling of leaves in the wind, the footsteps of the ants and the atoms' moving through the void. There is no screen that prevents the sound from reaching Him, nor is one sound heard less than the other when an almost infinite number of voices is speaking.

As-Samī', the All-Hearing, is an attribute of perfection, because its opposite, being deaf, is an imperfection. There

Allāh Mudhill, As-Samī, Al-Basīr, Al-Ḥakam

are two levels of perfection. One is absolute perfection, the other is relative perfection. Absolute perfection does not depend on means, conditions, or limitations. Relative perfection depends on means and conditions and is limited.

In the universe, from the beginning until the end, from one end to the other, without interruption, an almost endless number of sounds and voices exist. Some are as loud as the greatest explosion; some are minimal, almost imperceptible. All are heard by the All-Hearing—one by one at the same time, one as clear as the other. This hearing is not in vain, for all is registered: the meaning understood, the need satisfied, the answer given, the call responded to, the wrong corrected.

Of this infinite ability to hear, if an atom is given to man, it is in order that it guide man towards this absolute perfection. It is in order that he know His perfect attributes, which He has given in traces, in signs in and around us. It is so that we may know Him and find Him and love Him and be with Him. But when the ones who have the best ears and the most sensitive machinery listen—if they ever begin to compare their hearing to Allah the Hearer of All, they will be liars. Worse still, they will be guilty of *shirk*, attributing equals to Allah.

There is none like Him in any of His attributes and manifestations. The traces and signs of His attributes in man and upon the universe are at best a reflection, a symbol, a word, a means, a path to understand and reach truth.

'Abd as-Samī' and **'Abd al-Baṣīr** are the ones who hear and see the Truth with the eyes and ears of Allah, as Allah says in a divine Hadith: "My servant comes close to me with his continuous devotion until I love him and when I love him I become his ears with which he hears and his eyes with which he sees and his tongue with which he speaks and his hand with which he holds."

AL-BAṢĪR

البصير جل جلاله

He is the one who is All-Seeing.

He sees all that has passed, all there is and all there will be until the end of time—from the time when He moved the sea of nothingness in *'alam al-lāhūt* until after Doomsday and the Last Judgment. He has also given to His creatures the ability to behold His creation. Some of His creatures see shapes and colors and movements better than men do, but He has given man an eye of the heart, to see deeper than what meets the eye—an inner eye to see the inner man.

That eye is called the *baṣīrah.* Although we cannot see Allah—only He can see Himself—with the *baṣīrah* we can see ourselves. In doing so we will know that though we cannot see Him, He is looking at us, seeing not only what is on the outside of us, but what is in our minds and what is in our hearts. He who sees himself and knows himself knows that Allah sees him.

When you are in front of someone whom you respect and fear, you behave properly, with good conduct. You stand respectfully. You watch what you do and what you say. Yet that person can only see your outside; your respect and fear of him depend only on your temporal worldly interest and concern. The one who has created you and the ones before you, the one who truly controls your life, sustains you, loves you, protects you, has mercy on you, is with you night and day, the one on whom your life depends for eternity in the Hereafter—He is closer to you than your jugular vein. He has also told you clearly through His prophets and in His holy books what He wishes you to do, how He wishes you to behave, to the minutest detail. Yet right in front of His eyes, you do not hesitate to perform the most shameful and careless acts, without respect or fear.

Is it because you do not see Him that you believe that Allah al-Basir cannot see you?

AL-ḤAKAM

الحكم جل جلاله

He is the one who orders.

He is the bringer of justice and truth. He judges, and executes His justice. There is no justice but His. None can oppose His decree and none can prevent or delay the execution of His orders. He is the cause of the judged, the judge, the justice, and the judgment. All that happens in the universe is the effect of that one and only cause.

How can man, who is shortsighted, see the beginning and end of a chain of events? How often grandchildren pay for the sins of grandfathers, and fathers pay in advance for the sins of future generations! Do not judge Allah's justice. Often poison for one is medicine for another.

Allah has written His divine law in His holy books. Man understands it to the extent of his purity, sincerity, faith, knowledge, wisdom, and finally to the extent of his lot. Again according to his lot, man obeys or rebels and is rewarded or punished accordingly.

In Allah's attribute of the great Judge, *al-Ḥakam*, there are good tidings to the faithful, and a warning to the nonbelievers.

O believer, first be a true judge of yourself. Neither tyrannize yourself nor excuse and pamper yourself. Then judge others as you judge yourself. If you have any power to execute your judgment, make sure that your judgment is not other than Allah's decree and your power none other than that which is in His hand.

'Abd al-Ḥakam is he who executes Allah's judgement upon His servants as He wills.

AL-'ADL العَدْلُ جَلَّ جَلَالُهُ

His is the absolute justice. Justice is the opposite of tyranny. Tyranny causes pain, destruction, and disturbance. Justice secures peace, balance, order and harmony. Allah the Just is the enemy of tyrants; He hates those who support tyrants and their friends, sympathizers and acquaintances. In Islam, tyranny in any form or shape is unlawful. To be just is an honor and a distinction befitting a Muslim.

The opposites justice and tyranny have wide implications more important than their simple moral and social consequences. They are equated with harmony versus disharmony, order versus chaos, right against wrong. If in expression of his generosity someone gave money to the rich, swords to scholars and books to soldiers, he would, at one level, be considered a tyrant—for swords befit soldiers, books, scholars, and the poor need the money. Yet if Allah did the same His act would be justice—for He sees all, the before and the after, the inner and the outer. He is All-Knowing, the Beneficent, the Merciful, the Absolute Justice. He creates some beautiful and others ugly, some strong and others weak; then He renders the beautiful, ugly and the strong, weak; the rich, poor; the wise, dumb; the healthy, sick. All is just. All is right.

It seems to some unjust that there are those who are lame, blind, deaf, starving, insane, and that the young die.

Allah is the creator of the beautiful and of the ugly, the good as well as the bad. In this are mysteries difficult to understand. Yet we understand at least that one often needs to know the opposite of a thing in order to understand it. The one who has not experienced sadness cannot know happiness. If there were no ugliness we would be blind to beauty. Both good and bad are necessary. Allah shows one with the other, the right against the wrong, and shows us the consequences of each. He shows the rewards versus the punishments; then He leaves us free to use our own judgment. Each according to his lot may find salvation in misery and sickness, or damnation in riches. Allah knows what is best for His creation. Only Allah knows our destinies. The realization of destinies is His justice.

Out of respect for the beautiful name of Allah, *al-'Adl*, we must learn to exercise *shukr*, *tawakkul*, and *riḍa'*—thankfulness, trust in God, and acceptance. We must be thankful for the good, and accept, without personal judgment or complaint, whatever falls to our lot that does not seem to be good. In so doing, perhaps the mystery of Allah's justice will be revealed to you, and you will be happy with both the joy and the pain coming from the Beloved.

'Abd al-'Adl is the deputy of Allah in the manifestation of His justice. Divine justice is not equality as man imagines it to be. He gives the rights in right measure to the ones who have the right.

AL-LAṬĪF اللطيف جل جلاله

He is the most delicate, fine, gentle, beautiful one. He is the one who knows the finest details of beauty. He is the maker of a delicate beauty and the bestower of beauty upon His servants, for He is All-Beautiful. The finest of His beauties are hidden in the secrets of the beauties of the soul, the mind, wisdom, the divine light. He contains the minutest details of a divine puzzle where all things fit into each other. The fetus fits within the mother's womb, the pearl within the oyster, the fine silk within the silkworm, the honey in the bee, and in the heart of the human being, the knowledge of Allah Himself. But a heart that does not contain the beautiful light of knowing Allah, like a bee without honey, becomes a hornet with a poisonous stinger, stinging whoever comes close by.

Open your eyes of the heart and look hard to see the manifestations of *al-Laṭīf*. Sometimes it is a fine delicate mist of quietude within the turbulence of worldly activity. Sometimes it is a gentle blessing within His harsh punishment. Happy is he who can see, because for him there is no doubt, anxiety, or hopelessness.

'Abd al-Laṭīf is the one whose finer inner eye is opened to see the inner beauty in all. Thus he receives beauty himself and relates to all creation beautifully, rendering it beautiful. The exquisite beauty of Allah *al-Latīf* cannot be appreciated with our coarse eyes.

الخبير جلّ جلاله

AL-KHABĪR

He is the one who is aware of the hidden inner occurrences in everything. He is the one whose cognizance reaches the deepest, darkest, hidden corners of His kingdom, where neither human intelligence nor His angels can penetrate. Everywhere in the universe, an infinite number of things are happening, some universal, some minute, above and under, inside and outside each other. He is aware of all these from their very beginning until their end, with infinite detail. Occurrences which are not yet actualized, but in a state of formation or being planned and hidden, like secrets within secrets, are manifest to Him. None can escape His attention.

Know that there is nothing that you do in secret—or think of doing—that is not known by *al-Khabīr*. Know also that your most secret needs and wishes for which you have not asked in prayer are known to Him and are often accorded to you without your asking Him.

'Abd al-Khabīr is blessed with total understanding. He has been made aware, to know the before and the after, as well as the present, of occurrences.

AL-ḤALĪM الحليم جل جلاله

He is forbearing in the punishment of the guilty.

He waits, giving time to the sinner to realize his guilt and ask forgiveness in order that He may forgive him rather than punish him. He has absolute power and is just. Yet He is gentle and compassionate; He prefers to pardon the guilty rather than take vengeance.

So many among us deny Him, revolt against Him, disobey Him, tyrannize His good servants, mistreat His creation and tyrannize themselves. And they keep doing this, not even getting a bellyache from eating what is stolen from orphans. Do not think that they will go unpunished. Allah al-ʿAlim knows. Allah al-ʿAdl judges. But the gentle *al-Ḥalīm* waits, preferring to see them regret, change, repent, compensate for the harm they have done, so that He may forgive them and transform them into good servants rather than destroy them.

In this compassionate attribute of Allah there is a breath of relief for all of us. Is there a day or an hour that passes in which we have not sinned? If Allah were prompt in His punishment, not giving us time to realize what we have done and its consequences, to beg His forgiveness and hope for His mercy, there wouldn't be a man alive on the face of the earth.

Allah loves those pure and clean hearts that, like clear mirrors, reflect Allah's beautiful attributes. Allah loves the gentle *ḥalīm* man who is not ready to condemn, to avenge, but rather waits and hopes that his adversary will change and become *ḥalīm* himself.

ʿAbd al-Ḥalīm is blessed with perfect character. His manifestation is gentleness and forgiveness. Although having the power to punish and to take revenge, he will forgive and treat kindly the ones who tyrannize him. He will be forbearing in the face of the treachery of the deceitful and the stupidity of the vile. Yet he is always victorious over the mean with his gentleness.

AL-'AẒĪM

العظيم جل جلاله

He is the Greatest—on the earth below and in the heavens above, in realms where our sight cannot reach and of which our minds cannot conceive. His is the absolute and perfect greatness. The greatness we know is all relative, and all of it is a witness to His being the Greatest. No greatness can be compared to His. The greatest thing we are able to know still has needs. How could the absolute Greatest have needs? Allah al-'Azim has no needs. He is the satisfier of all needs.

We call some among us great. Greatness, in man, depends upon one's work, one's achievement. We call some among these great ones "greatest"—those whose work is greatest. The work of these is nothing in comparison to the billions of greater works of Allah al-'Azim. The greatest man is one of Allah's works. The greatest work that he has done is one of Allah's works. Allah's humblest work, a blade of grass with its pulsating cells transforming the earth, the water, the air, the light of the sun into life, color, and sustenance for all His other works—all this is a factory containing mysteries that no botanist could venture to imagine. For seeing the greatness of the Greatest, that blade of grass is a witness vast enough to surpass our comprehension. You who cannot even understand the mystery in the creation of that blade of grass must compare it to countless other things visible and invisible, reachable with all your telescopes and microscopes, unknowable in your wildest imagination, to see His greatness.

In your minuteness and awe, you must prostrate and glorify Him, and pray to be included among those servants who meet His pleasure and are accepted by Him.

'Abd al-'Aẓīm is he to whom Allah appears in His perfect greatness. And from the power generating from the right he sees to the condemnation of the ones who oppose the right. He appears above others in magnificence and strength as his inner greatness is reflected in his outer appearance.

AL-GHAFŪR

الغفور جل جلاله

He is the most forgiving one. An aspect of forgiveness is to hide our faults and treat them as if they had never existed.

There are three meanings to the forgiveness of Allah, three separate divine attributes—*al-Ghaffār*, *al-Ghāfir*, and *al-Ghafūr*.

Al-Ghāfir is His quality of hiding His servants' shameful acts in order that they be able to live with each other, have faith in each other, and be able to depend on, love and respect each other. Otherwise, if Allah al-Ghafir in His mercy did not hide our faults, our adverse opinions, ugly thoughts and hateful feelings, everyone would run away from everyone else. There could be neither a society nor a single family.

Next Allah al-Ghafur hides our faults in the realms of the spirit and of angels just as He does in this world. The angels see things we cannot see in this world. Allah hides our faults from them so that we will not be ashamed in the Hereafter. Through this name we may find the same respect and closeness from the spirits and the angels—from whom our sins are hidden by Allah al-Ghafur—that His forgiveness permitted us among men.

Allah's name *al-Ghaffār* is the most encompassing in forgiveness. A man whose faults are hidden from others is saved from being ashamed in front of them, but he may still be ashamed of himself within himself. Everyone has a degree of conscience which suffers from his actions. Allah al-Ghaffar in His mercy hides man's faults even from himself and makes him forget in order to alleviate his suffering.

Remember *al-Ghāfir*, the veiler of our faults from the eyes of other men; *al-Ghafūr*, who keeps the knowledge of our faults even from the angels; and *al-Ghaffār*, who relieves us from the suffering of continual remembrance of our faults. To such a compassionate one should we not be thankful? Should we not confess our sins, repenting with tears in our eyes, asking His forgiveness?

'Abd al-Ghafūr is the forgiver of wrongs and the hider of faults.

الشكور جل جلاله

ASH-SHAKŪR

He is the one who repays a good deed with a much greater reward. Thankfulness is to return good with good. To be thankful is a duty of man towards Allah. He is the one who created you and poured upon you all His bounties. He has left you free to see His gifts and to be thankful, or to be blinded by arrogance, denying even His existence.

Blessed is the one who chooses the path of thankfulness, spending what Allah bestows upon him in Allah's way. Then Allah ash-Shakur returns his thankfulness with rewards infinitely superior to his good deeds, and this in turn paves the way for further good deeds.

The thankful one knows that all he is and all he has is from Allah. He uses every part of his body—his mind, his tongue, his hands—only for the purposes for which they were created. He uses all that he has—his talents, his strength, his money—for Allah's pleasure on Allah's creation. Allah helps the thankful and increases their wisdom, their abilities, and their fortunes.

The ones who deny the bounties of Allah and hide them in secret rooms all for themselves are misers who pretend that they do not have anything. Therefore, although they have a lot, it is just as if they have nothing, so they want more and more. Never finding enough, they suffer destitution in the midst of abundance. Allah leaves them alone with their egos, their insatiable greed. All the bounties that they have received decay, stored in some secret place, unused. They pass from one loss to another, from one disaster to a worse one. If they do not take heed of these lessons, their unthankfulness will lead them to eternal damnation. We take refuge in Allah from such an eventuality.

'Abd ash-Shakūr sees all good and nothing but good, and that all good comes from Allah. He is in a state of continuous thankfulness as was Hz. 'Ali (May Allah be pleased with him), who said: "All praise and thanks to Allah who presents His greatest favors to His beloved servants in the form of hardship and affliction, and presents to His enemies His punishment in the form of bounties."

AL-'ALĪ

العلي جل جلاله

He is the Highest One. He is higher than the whole of the created universe. This does not mean that His highness is closer to the high mountains, to the stars above, to the higher intellects or to the ones who occupy high positions. Neither is He farther from the deepest depths and the lowest of the low. He is close to every atom of His creation in all places, and closer to man than his jugular vein.

As His essence and attributes do not bear any resemblance to the essence and attributes of His created beings. His nearness and farness and His being high cannot be measured by the limits of human intellect.

He is higher than the unimaginable heights. None resemble Him. He is higher than all perfect attributes in power,

Ya 'Alī, Ya Kabīr

knowledge, judgment and will together. *Al-'Alī* is He who is highest by Himself, in Himself, in the qualification that applies only to Him.

Some, with good will but lesser mental and spiritual comprehension, think of Allah as a Being residing in high heavens on His throne, and imagine Him as if king of a vast kingdom, ruling the universe through His agents, officers, priests and potentates.

Allah Most High has no place, for He is the place of all places.

He has no time, as He is the time of all times.

He needs no agent to act in His name.

He is the highest in the sense that He is above and encompasses all that has been, all there is, and all there will be.

'Abd al-'Alī is he who is valued by all because he is given virtue and generosity, and who supports and helps all those around him.

AL-KABĪR

الكبير جل جلاله

He is the Greatest, whose greatness stretches from before the beginning until after the end. The greatness of all conceivable greatnesses from the beginning to the end is only His creation and is proof of His greatness.

We use the term "infinite" in relation to the heavens and to time. This attribution of infinity to created things is only because a proper conception of them will not fit into our understanding. If we had a vehicle as fast as our thoughts and our imagination, and if we were carried in it in a straight line, in one direction, into the depths of the heavens, across immeasurable distances, passing millions of suns in every second, and if we had a life of billions of centuries, we would travel through only a very little of the created universe and created time.

All this which cannot fit into our comprehension was created with a single word and with His will. If He so wills, He could do it again and again and more and more without losing any of His strength. There is no difference for Him between the creation of an atom and the infinite-seeming universe. This is His grandeur as much as we can understand it. He is greater than that.

The realization of His grandeur should raise in us the fear and love of Him, and the wish to be nothing but His servants. Fear of Him is not the fear of a tyrannical strength that could crush one, whether rightfully, in vengeance, or arbitrarily. He is the Merciful, the Compassionate, the Wise, the Just, the Generous, the Loving. The fear of Allah is a fear that is an outcome of loving Him—wishing to be loved by Him and fearing to lose His love, to face His disappointment in you. The greatest loss for man is to receive Allah's disappointment and anger, and the greatest gain for man is to be the beloved of Allah.

How much effort do we spend for the approval and love that we hope to receive from those whom we consider great! What a loss of effort to seek the love of the servant instead of the Master!

'Abd al-Kabīr grows and is perfected by the hand of Allah alone, without any effort on his own or support from others.

الحفيظ جل جلاله

AL-ḤAFĪẒ

He is the one who remembers all that was and all that is, keeping in His divine protection all that there will be.

He is aware of, remembers, and keeps in His memory all that you do, or say, and think at all times. He preserves all; nothing is lost. In His preservation, there is also protection.

He protects His creation from all harm and disharmony. That is how all the heavenly bodies speeding in great haste revolve and travel within their destined orbits, instead of clashing with each other. As a manifestation of His name *al-Ḥafīẓ*, He has placed in each of His creations an instinct for survival. He protects man by teaching that that which is bad for him is unlawful. Lawful food, aged and spoiled, becomes unlawful. Lawful bread, burnt and carbonized, becomes unlawful. They have turned into poison.

So the poisons of alcohol, adultery, gambling and gossip are unlawful, and arrogance, hypocrisy, envy and ignorance are poisons to one's spiritual being. As a blessing of *al-Ḥafīẓ*, the Protector, Allah has sent His prophets, His books, His teachers, to teach wisdom, intelligence, the divine law to protect man from material and spiritual harm. But the ones who are heedless of Allah, His prophets and His books, who disbelieve and revolt—they are thankless. With their own small will they turn away from the protection and preservation of Allah. So Allah does not treat them with His attribute of *al-Ḥafīẓ*, but with His attribute of *ar-Raqīb*, the Watcher who responds according to one's actions.

Use well Allah's means of preservation and protection which he has bestowed upon you. Protect yourself from evil, from revolt, from sin; help and protect others; remember and preserve Allah's words in His Holy Qur'an, His sacred law, and the words of His prophets, and help others to do the same.

'Abd al-Ḥafīẓ is protected in all his states, actions, words, outwardly and inwardly, by Allah the Protector. The protection of Allah over him is so strong that the ones who are close to him, who are around him, who know or touch him are also protected. It is said that the friends and acquaintances of Hz. Abu Sulayman Darani (May Allah be pleased with him) who stayed in his company for thirty years never suffered adversity, nor did a bad thought ever come to their minds, nor a negative feeling come to their hearts during that time.

AL-MUQĪT

المُقِيتُ جَلَّ جَلَالُهُ

He is the Nourisher of all creation.

Allah creates the nourishment of each of His creatures before He creates them. No one can take away the nourishment destined for each element of the creation.

The sustenance due to one will not run out until death overtakes him. Look at the plants, look at the birds. Think of the twins in the womb of the mother, how each takes its destined nourishment without trying to take away from the other and without fighting. Yet the same twins who tranquilly and peacefully received their sustenance through their mother's lifeblood, coming into this world and growing up, may kill each other for the inheritance of their mother. Has Allah told them, "When you come into the world, go and fetch your own sustenance, I am done with you"? Has He forgotten to give them their sustenance?

Allah is *'Alīm*. He is *Khabīr*. He does not forget. He does not fall into error. He is *Qayyūm*, *Muhaymin*, the Lord of the Universes. He does not lose sight of His creation, nor does He fail in His protection and care for it even for a split second.

He gives nourishment without being asked to the ones who cannot ask and work for their own nourishment. For the ones who can, Allah has created means of sustenance. He needs no means. Because Allah wills it, His servants may choose between lawful and unlawful means.

Opting for the unlawful will not increase your sustenance. Whatever your nourishment is and wherever you receive it, it can only be your lot. The means do not create the sustenance. They do not even give the sustenance. The means are like pipes coming from Allah the Nourisher to each and every creation. The nourishment in them flows as death presses from the end of the pipes. Death will not come upon you until your nourishment is finished, and it will certainly come upon you after your last mouthful and breath.

Therefore a faithful servant of Allah, who believes that Allah al-Muqit is the creator and giver of his nourishment until the day of his death, counts on Allah's promise alone. He opts for the lawful means. He does not endanger his life here and in the Hereafter with evil ambition, treachery, and lying to try to get the sustenance due to others.

'Abd al-Muqīt is given the awareness of the needs of others and the means to satisfy those needs at the right time in the right amount without delay and with nothing lacking.

AL-ḤASĪB

He is the one who takes account of all and everything that His creation does or is subjected to.

There are certain affairs and concepts that can be expressed in numbers. To reach a conclusion certain calculations are necessary. The conclusion of most of the affairs of the created universe necessitates such calculation. But Allah knows the result of all without any need for such operations because His knowledge does not depend on any causes or means, nor upon any analysis or thought.

On the Day of Last Judgment man will have to present his accounting to Allah. That is why that day is also called the Day of Reckoning. We will have to give the accounting of all that we have received and how we have spent it. Billions and billions of others like us will appear on the same day. Allah is such an accountant that He knows even the number of breaths taken from the first man He created to the last man whom He will take to Himself. On that day, we will have to give the accounting of all the capital Allah has lent us.

The greatest capital that He has lent us is our life. Whatever we will gain, we will gain with that. Our capital is being spent day by day, hour by hour. With each breath, the time of the final accounting is closer. We have to return the capital of this temporary life to its owner. We will be rewarded for the gains and be responsible for the losses. Some will have gone bankrupt: the nonbelievers who have squandered Allah's capital.

Know that every minute that passes without benefit—every hour you are not working for Allah's sake, caring for His creation or remembering Him, thanking Him, praising Him, watching what you are doing—is a loss. You have no hope ever to regain that loss; you cannot buy back yesterday, even if you spend the rest of your life. Know the value of your life. Don't squander it in laziness, in heedlessness and in dreams. Make your calculations now before you have to present your accounting to Allah al-Hasib.

'Abd al-Ḥasîb watches over the good use of life, means, sustenance and everything else which Allah has given to His creation in limited amounts. He sees to the good management of Allah's bounties upon His creatures.

AL-JALĪL

الجليل جل جلاله

He is the Lord of Majesty and Might. His might and His greatness, His eternity bear no resemblance to any energy, matter or time. His essence, His attributes, His very existence are mighty and great; they are immeasurable in time, nor do they fit into any space, yet He is here, everywhere, at all times.

His knowledge is great; all is known to Him as He created all. His power is great; it encompasses all universes and each atom. His mercy is great; He forgives all. His generosity is limitless, His treasures inexhaustible. Whom should we respect, praise, love and obey but the Mighty, the Great?

Who is the Mighty and the Great? The one who is powerful, who is wise, who is generous, who is compassionate. Even someone who possessed one of these characteristics would be considered great.

Allah is the owner and source of all attributes of greatness, known and unknown. He is the one who distributes specks of greatness to whatever and whomever He wishes in His creation. He is the owner of all good and perfection, the goal of all hopes.

Existence, life, death, gain and loss, all are His will. The mind, the heart, the soul, the whole being of one who knows this, are filled with His love and fear. Through loving Him, he also loves the ones whom He loves, the ones who love Him, the ones who teach His words and the words that they teach. All love is due to Him.

'Abd al-Jalīl casts fear in everyone's hearts, as Allah has given him a share of His majesty and might.

AL-KARĪM

الكريم جل جلاله ١٧

He is the Generous One. His greatest generosity is His mercy, through which He forgives when He could punish. He fulfills His promises. He has promised rewards for good deeds. In His generosity, His rewards surpass all expectations. He also promises punishment for the sinner. That is called *al-wa'īd*, the threat, in accordance with which all who sin should expect punishment. Yet He in His divine judgment finds extenuating circumstances, and in His generosity, forgives.

He is generous to those who take refuge in Him. You need not seek intermediaries to stand in His presence. He knows your difficulties and your needs before you know them yourself. In His generosity He gives help, satisfying your needs even before you ask.

The generous among men are those who have been the recipients of more of Allah's generosity than others; that gift is generosity itself. Those are the people who are not content when they are not able to give or to help others.

The generous among men do not always receive recognition or thanks; on the contrary, they are bothered with increased demands. Petitioners from far and near crowd around them. The generous one should be thankful, and know that this is a sign that Allah has accepted the services of His servant, and has increased his honor.

One should not tire, one should not be proud. Those are the dangers. For the ones in need, hopelessness and doubt of the generosity of Allah are also dangers. It is also dangerous for the sinner, no matter how enormous his sin, to doubt Allah's mercy and His generosity.

'Abd al-Karīm is a witness to the infinite generosity of Allah and acts in accordance with it. He is able to fully appreciate Allah's generosity, knowing that none of that which is given to us is ours. Whoever receives it is unworthy and certainly does not deserve it, yet as Allah hides our faults and weaknesses, so does 'Abd al-Karim overlook our faults and hide them from others. As Allah forgives our unthankfulness, so does he. Allah says in Surah Infitar (v. 6-7): "Oh man, what beguiles thee from thy Lord, the Generous who created thee, then made thee complete, then made thee in the best of states?" It is said that when Hz.'Umar (May Allah be pleased with him) heard these verses, he answered Allah's question by saying: "It is your generosity itself, Oh my Lord." Hz. Muhyiddin ibn al-'Arabi says that this comment of Hz. 'Umar has as its purpose to attract others' attention to their spoiled state. Compared to the immeasurable bounties of Allah the Generous, the sins and the revolt of the servant become minute and inconsequential. The servant in whom He manifests His graciousness knows no bound to his gifts and no fault in the ungratefulness of those who take his gifts.

AR-RAQĪB

الرقيب جل جلاله

He is the one who watches everything, always.

This scrutiny of every detail in the existence of all creation is in part protective. Allah watches His faithful servants proceeding on their allotted paths in harmony with each other and everything else, and protects them from the intentions and the actions of those who revolt, who are about to clash with what is rightful.

The ones under the watchful eye of *ar-Raqīb*, who are heedful, aware, obedient, serving Allah for Allah's sake, should know that not a speck of their good deeds will be lost; all will be rewarded. The heedless ones who dream that they are their own masters and that they can do and have all that they want should know that not one of their moves against the divine order and harmony will pass unnoticed and unpunished.

In accordance with this attribute of Allah, man should realize that in addition to Allah ar-Raqib, the loving merciful watcher, there are two other watchers, deadly enemies who watch you all the time to find an appropriate time and a weak spot to attack you; to possess, to torture, to kill you. These two wakeful enemies are the accursed Devil and the insatiable egoist, the *nafs*.

You must will all the awareness within your power, and watch every minute the moves of these enemies who have surrounded you from four sides and from the inside.

'Abd ar-Raqib is more aware of Allah watching him and everything than he is aware of his very existence. That is why he is unable to cross the borders of Allah's prescriptions. None other than the one blessed by the manifestation of this name is totally conscious and totally in control of himself and others around him. In reality, he is an expression of Allah's watching over him and others.

AL-MUJĪB المجيب جل جلاله

He is the one who responds to all the prayers or needs of His servants. Allah is closer to His creatures than they are to themselves. His proximity to all His creation is the same. He is not any closer to a saint than He is to you or to a mustard seed. He knows the needs of His creation before they realize them, and gives their satisfaction even before it is needed.

It is the manifestation of *al-Mujīb* in man that we be attentive and responsive above all to Allah, the one who created us and furnishes all our needs, by glorifying Him and by begging for our needs from Him, by attending to our duties prescribed by Him, and by responding to the needs of His other creatures when Allah chooses to give through our hands.

'Abd al-Mujīb is the one who obeys and accepts Allah's call when he hears Allah say in Surah Ahqaf (v.31): "Oh our people, accept the inviter to Allah and believe in him." As he accepts Allah's call, Allah accepts his call and that is when His attribute *al-Mujīb*, the One who responds to His servant's call, is expressed in His servant. When *'Abd al-Mujīb* calls, all come; as he has responded to Allah, all respond to him. Allah confirms this in Surah Baqarah (v.186): "And when My servants ask thee concerning Me, surely I am near. I answer the prayer of the supplicant when he calls upon Me. So should they hear My call and believe in me, that they may walk in the right way."

AL-WĀSI' الواسع جل جلاله

He is the limitless vastness, whose knowledge, mercy, power, generosity, and all other beautiful attributes are infinite.

Al-Wāsi' is also interpreted as the endlessness of the tolerance of Allah. The wrongs and sins of man are like a drop of dirt in the vastness of Allah's ocean of tolerance. A sign of *al-Wāsi'* is in the infinite variety of His creations. Look at man: although we are all made of the same material, no two faces, no two voices are alike.

The all-reaching vastness of Allah is reflected in man—in men of vast knowledge from whom many benefit, in men of great riches and greater generosity who help the needy far and wide; in men of compassion, gentleness and great patience whose far-reaching justice inspires great confidence. All other unconditional and limitless good qualities in men are reflections of *al-Wāsi'*.

Know that Allah's knowledge is vast, reaching all, everywhere. You cannot hide anything from Him. His power is overwhelming; nothing can escape it, so beware of sinning and revolting. His mercy is infinite, so turn to Him. He is tolerant in His commandments, and forgiving, so do not lose hope.

'Abd al-Wāsi' has a wisdom which is all-inclusive. His being covers all possible levels to which a human being may aspire to rise. He is vast and cannot be limited within any restrictions.

AL-ḤAKĪM

الحكيم جل جلاله

He is the perfectly wise, in His knowledge and in His deeds.

There is no doubt or uncertainty in His knowledge, nor does it have an end. Neither is there any doubt or uncertainty in His commandments. Whoever follows them will learn from the reflection of His perfect knowledge that which he knew not, and evolve towards being a perfect man. Whoever will not follow Allah's orders will receive neither good nor benefit; he will not grow but will dry up, becoming fuel for Hellfire.

Look at all the things Allah forbade you. Each of them is a calamity. Allah created these calamities and the unlawful as well as the lawful. He forbade the former and permitted the latter. He is the one who gave you the force to obey and the weakness to disobey. He left you free to choose. This test is not to show Him whether you are faithful or faithless. Allah knew all about you before He created you. The test is for you and for others, so that you yourself and others know you.

None of Allah's deeds are without benefit and wisdom. None of Allah's wisdom and deeds are for Allah's benefit. Allah needs nothing. The purpose of this wisdom is the order and continuity of the cosmos until the appointed time.

Look at your inner being, a microcosm, a model for the universe. See how every organ, every cell is perfectly created for a definite function, how everything without fail works harmoniously. The purpose of this wisdom of perfect cooperation is only to keep that being alive until the appointed time.

The totality of the knowledge of what keeps you—your body, your mind, your soul—alive, is man's portion of *al-Ḥakīm*. When you see that, you will see the mark of Allah's wisdom in you.

'Abd al-Ḥakīm is shown the secrets of the reason of creation and as he knows the purpose of each creation, his behavior and actions towards them are in accordance with that knowledge. When he sees a deviation from the purpose, he is able to correct it.

AL-WADŪD

الودود جل جلاله

He is the one who loves His good servants. He is the only one who is worthy of love.

Allah in His infinite and unconditional love of His good servants has given them all ability, but above all the ability to love Him. He has given them the possibility to receive and achieve Truth, which is beyond the understanding of ordinary intellect. *Fayḍ* is that special ability.

This in itself is not sufficient. To be able to profit from this enlightenment, *fayḍ*, there is yet another condition, which is faith, and faith put into action, which is devotion. Let the ones who seek enlightenment run to piety and worship.

Al-Wadūd is that sole goal of the heart which seeks the love of Allah. But love is only possible if the lover is aware of the beloved, as well as of the beauty and perfection of the beloved.

For most people, awareness depends on their senses, and the senses are many. Each one is attracted to different things. When the soul is aware of itself and one is aware of one's soul, then the senses follow the soul which is aware of the whole. Allah is the sole Beloved of the soul, because all perfection is in Him. All the senses are ecstatic with the inexhaustible sweet taste of this perfection.

How does one reach that state of sensitivity and awareness when the flesh naturally loves its good life, its pleasures, health, home, property, business, and so forth? No ordinary man needs education, intelligence, incentive and guidance to love these things. But to love Allah, he does need at least intelligence and guidance in order to realize that all he naturally loves is Allah's possession and His gift, that all this is a sign of His care and love for him.

All that he loves is temporary, as he himself is. Only his sacred soul, the greatest gift to him, and the Owner of that soul, his Creator, are eternal. The realization of this is a much greater gift than all one could possess in this world. For when Allah loves His servant, He gives him understanding, consciousness, faith and love of Him.

The *wadūd* among men is he who loves for others that which he loves for himself. Indeed, he prefers the needs of others to his own. Such a blessed one has said, "I pray that I be stretched over the whole of Hell so that the feet of sinners do not burn."

Even when one suffers at the hands of those for whom one wishes more than one wishes for oneself, one should say, as the Beloved of Allah (Peace and Blessings of Allah be upon him) said when he was wounded in the battle of Uhud, "O my Lord, guide my tribe well, for they don't know what they are doing, they do not know the Truth."

'Abd al-Wadūd is the one whose love for Allah and the ones who love Allah is perfected. When Allah loves his servant, he spreads the love for that servant far and wide so that all, except the heedless, love him too. Muhammad, the beloved of Allah (Peace and Blessings of Allah be upon him) says: "When Allah loves a servant He calls the archangel Gabriel (May Allah bless him) and says, 'I love this servant of Mine, love him also.' Then Gabriel (May Allah bless him) calls unto the heavens and says, 'Oh all those who are in the heavens, Allah loves this servant, love him too.' So all that exist in the heavens love him. Then the love of that servant is proposed to the creatures of the earth and they love him also."

Ya Razzāq, Ya ʿAlīm, Ya Ḥakīm, Ya Wadūd, Ya Majīd

المجيد جل جلاله

AL-MAJĪD

He is the Most Majestic and Glorious.

Allah Most High is glorious and majestic in the whole of His creation and beyond. No hand reaches Him, no power can touch Him, yet He is closer to His servants than their own souls; He has love and mercy for them more than they could have for themselves. His bounties are infinite; there is no end to His mercy. His state is pure perfection; His acts are pure wisdom.

In the meaning of *al-Majīd* there are two elements. One is His Majesty, His Power, which keeps Him over and above any attempt to reach Him, and for which He is respected and feared. The other is His Glory and Honor shown in His beautiful actions and states, for which He is praised and loved.

It behooves the good servant, in consideration of the glory and honor of his Lord, to be sincere, serious, and pure in his devotions to Him, as well as in all his doings, thereby seeking His pleasure. He should recoil from arrogance, hypocrisy and lies. Those who realize the majesty and the honor of their Lord, who believe, and who join Him, seeking only His pleasure, receive strength and honor themselves.

'Abd al-Majīd is the one whose character and morals are perfected. He is honored amongst men and the rest of creation because of his beautiful behavior towards them. He is virtuous by the virtues of Allah.

AL-BĀ'ITH

الْبَاعِثُ جَلَّ جَلَالُهُ

He is the raiser from the dead.

Allah al-Ba'ith will give life back to all creation on the Day of Last Judgment. He will raise people from their graves and bring out all the actions, thoughts, and feelings that occurred during their lifetimes on this earth. This attribute of Allah is so important that it is one of the seven affirmations, the last condition of faith, for the faithful one must declare that he believes that he will be brought back to life after death. This is true. It is real. It certainly will happen. Allah has made this Truth known in all the books He has revealed and through all the prophets whom He has sent. In the Holy Qur'an, almost all the chapters have some mention of it.

> And the Hour is coming, there is no doubt about it; and Allah will raise up those who are in the graves.
>
> (The Pilgrimage, v. 7)
>
> From it [earth] We created you, and into it We shall return you, and from it raise you a second time.
>
> (Ta Ha, v. 55)
>
> Allah is He Who created you, then He sustained you, then He causes you to die, then brings you to life.
>
> (The Romans, v. 40)

How is one to realize the meaning of *al-Bā'ith* while one thinks that one comes to this life from nothing and nowhere, and one goes after death to nothing and nowhere? Death is not "nothing," neither is the revival after death like one's birth. After death, there is the life of the tomb, which is either a pit of the fire of Hell or a rose garden from the rose gardens of Paradise. The dead are either tortured beings in misery or blessed beings in bliss, but they are not dead and gone into nothingness.

The Messenger of Allah (Peace and Blessings of Allah be upon him) stood on the edge of the pit where the enemies of Allah who had fought him at the battle of Badr were buried, and said in a loud voice, "I have seen now that [victory] which my Lord promised me come to be. Are you also seeing the punishment which your Lord promised you?" When his followers asked him, "How could you talk with those who are dead and gone?" the Messenger of Allah (Peace and Blessings of Allah be upon him) said, "They hear what I say to them better than you can, only they are not able to answer."

And Allah, addressing the martyrs of the battle of Uhud, revealed the following ayats:

> And think not of those who are killed in Allah's way as dead. Nay, they are alive being provided sustenance from their Lord. Rejoice in what Allah has given them out of His grace, and they rejoice for the sake of those who, [being left] behind them, have not yet joined them, that they have no fear, nor shall they grieve.
>
> (Al 'Imran, v. 168-169)

Birth is not like the revival after death. Neither are coming to this world and coming back after death the only instances of receiving life. There are many revivals, each different, occurring frequently in life. That is why Allah says, "We recreate you in places where you do not suspect."

Within this life are many deaths and revivals. How often the soul loses its control of the flesh and again regains control. It even happens medically: people die and are revived. Within your body, cells are continually dying and new ones are being born. Don't you see that in all these cases what dies and is revived is only the flesh? The soul is eternal.

To deny things that he has not experienced, that he does not know, is in man's nature. Because in this life he has not experienced the Hereafter, nor coming to life after death, he does not believe. A child who has not come to the age of discernment and who has not yet burnt his hand will refuse to believe that the fire is hot. If he believes his mother and does not touch the fire, he is a happy baby. He who has faith in things he has not experienced and which he cannot understand is he who has faith in the unseen. This is the key to bliss.

Do not be of the unfaithful, like Ubayy ibn Khalaf, who crushed decayed old bones between his fingers and threw them in our Master's (Peace and Blessings of Allah be upon him) face, saying, "So you claim that He will revive these rotten bones?"

The Prophet (Peace and Blessings of Allah be upon him) said, "Indeed, so will He recreate you so that He will put you in His fire."

On this occasion, the following ayats were revealed:

> . . . Says he, Who will give life to the bones when they are rotten? Say: He will give life to them, who brought them into existence at first, and He is knower of all creation.
>
> (Ya Sin, v. 78-79)

Allah's promise of your being brought back to life on the Day of Last Judgment is sure. You are going to die the way you live; you are going to be revived the way you die. Whatever you sow here, you will reap in the Hereafter. Choose the seeds of good deeds. Till the ground with your efforts. Water your seeds with your tears of love and compassion and warm your fields with the divine light reflected upon the mirror of your clean heart. Do not forget that Allah in His Holy Qur'an likened *'ilm*, knowledge, to *ḥayyāt*, life, and *jahl*, ignorance, to *mawāt*, death. Whoever revives himself from the death of ignorance into the life of knowledge, or whoever helps another to be reborn into knowledge from the dark tomb of ignorance, will then see the manifestation of *al-Bā'ith* and truly believe it.

'Abd al-Bā'ith is the one whose egotism, lust, desires of the flesh and the love of the world have been killed, and whose heart has been purified and revived to eternal life. He has "died before dying" and he is able to revive, through his knowledge and wisdom, the dead hearts which have been killed with ignorance.

ASH-SHAHĪD الشَّهِيدُ جَلَّ جَلَالُهُ

He is the one who witnesses all that happens everywhere at all times.

Allah is close to all things, whether one attributes nearness or farness to them. He witnesses all things and events, whether large or small. He knows everything through His attribute *al-'Alīm*. He knows the secrets and the inner aspects of everything through His attribute *al-Khabīr*, and He is a witness to everything that appears, whether there are other witnesses or not, through His attribute *ash-Shahīd*. He is going to be the witness on the final Day of Judgment for every action of every man.

Ibn Mas'ud (May Allah be pleased with him) went with some of the Companions for a stroll into the country near Medina, where they saw a child shepherding a flock. They invited him to share their meal. The boy declined, saying that he was fasting. This excessive devotion amazed the Companions, as it was not the month of Ramadan. Partly as a pleasantry and partly as a test, they asked the boy to sell them a sheep, and promised him half of its meat as a gift. The boy said that the sheep were not his and he did not have the right to sell them. Then, with the intention of testing him, they said, "My son, who will know? You can always say that you lost a sheep." At that the boy screamed *ayn Allāh?*—Where is Allah?—and ran away. As a reward, Ibn Mas'ud (May Allah be pleased with him) bought the herd from its owner and donated it to the young shepherd, who thus profited already in the world for his awareness of *ash-Shahīd*. Ibn Mas'ud, as he met the young shepherd from time to time in Medina, would tease him by asking him, "Where is Allah?"

'Abd ash-Shahīd witnesses the truth of everything as well as the absolute Truth, and sees that he, as well as all else, is under the will of that Absolute Truth.

AL-ḤAQQ الْحَقُّ

Allah is the Truth, whose being is ever unchanged.

Haqq is that whose essence is valid in itself, and whose essence is the cause and is necessary for all other existence. As He does not gain His existence from other than Himself, He is eternal. Everything else is temporal; since *Ḥaqq* is existent by itself, not influenced by any other, He is non-changing. He is the only true existence. Other existences which appear truly to exist take the truth of their existence from Him.

There are other things in existence that are seen by the intellect as corresponding to that Truth. We call these "truth" as well. Yet the truths of all other existences change in their relationship to each other, and finally, when they disappear, the belief in their being true becomes invalid.

There is nothing in creation whose existence is parallel to that of Allah, the Truly Existent, who is forever before the before and after the after. The creation is likened to the moon: at the beginning a fine bow, as thin as a string; then a crescent; a full moon; then reversing and disappearing again. This is the order of the universe. Everything except Allah the Truly Existent begins, changes, disappears, reappears.

The manifestation of the attribute *al-Ḥaqq* appears for the believer in faith and in words. The truth is that which needs no proof, and whose denial is impossible. So the beliefs and words relating to the non-changing causal existence are called "true faiths" and "true words," because they too in a manner of speaking are constant. Allah keeps them constant and alive, and rewards the ones who speak them, listen to them and believe in them.

'Abd al-Ḥaqq has been saved from all falsehood, in his actions and in his words. He is aware of the truth at all times, everywhere; and through that, of the unity and oneness of all—as the Truth is, for him, ever-present and constant.

AL-WAKĪL

الْوَكِيلُ جَلَّ جَلَالُهُ

Allah is the ultimate and faithful trustee. He completes the work left to Him without leaving anything undone.

Men think that they are able to do, but He is the one who does everything and He has no need for anyone to do things for Him. He can replace everything in the universe, but nothing can replace Him nor can stand on its own without being dependent on Him. Neither His messengers nor His prophets are His trustees. He only manifests His messages and His trusteeship through them. They are His servants; He is the Lord and the Owner of all.

He does best everything that is left to Him, yet He is under no obligation. None can influence His will; no power can force Him to do a thing. He does for you what is good for you, and that which pleases Him.

Who is the one whom you may trust to do for you better than you can do for yourself? The trustee has to know better. He has to be more powerful. He has to be trustworthy. Someone who entrusts his affairs to another has to be sure of all that. He also has to have confidence in the compassion, love and loyalty of the trustee for him. Who among men is such a lawyer to represent you, and work for you? What payment are you prepared to give for the services of such a trustee? No man is such a trustee. When men do things for each other, it is only a business transaction; they give and they take. Allah, the All-Knowing, the All-Powerful, the Most Compassionate, is the only one for His servants to trust.

In all we pretend to do, in our business, for the maintenance of our health, for our family, for our children, we seek a benefit, we plan, we calculate, we take precautions, we consult with accountants, doctors, lawyers; yet daily all sorts of unforeseen hindrances, oppositions, and problems appear. The true servant does all this the best he can, not only for himself, but for others. Then he leaves the outcome for Allah in His bounty to give to him. He prays to *al-Wakīl*, whose hand controls his life, to do that which is good for him, as he himself admits that he knows not. This is the meaning of *tawakkul*, to trust in Allah. He who has this absolute trust in the ultimate and faithful Trustee owns a greater treasure than the greatest treasures of this world, because even in the total loss of his efforts he does not fall into despair; he is at peace. If that peace is nonexistent, no worldly benefit, no material treasure is going to bring happiness.

The difficulties that prevent or destroy this peace of mind are excessive ambition, miserliness, competitiveness, fear, and imagination. No amount of money, no amount of security, is going to relieve the constricted hearts of those afflicted by these sicknesses.

Tawakkul, trust in Allah, does not mean ignoring the causes of things that happen. To sit and not care about the causes and their effects is laziness. Trust in Allah is an obligation in Islam, and laziness is a sin. Allah has revealed to His servants the causes and the solutions of things that will happen. In fact, He has made the realization of these causes and solutions a condition for these things to happen. For a thing to be created, for a need to be satisfied, a reason, a cause, has to appear. This is Allah's law and order, called *ḥikmat al-tasbīb*, causal reason. To ignore what is available to one is purposefully to throw oneself into the jaws of the dragon of ignorance, sickness and poverty, which is unlawful and sinful according to Islam.

Thus, well aware of the causes, one should strive for what one wishes, knowing that all one's effort is but an active prayer, a wish for Allah's help. Indeed, these active prayers of your efforts become a proof of your trust in Allah for the outcome, and nothing more. He who does this does not count on his efforts but counts on Allah the Beneficent who says, "Ask and I will give."

ʿAbd al-Wakīl is the servant who becomes the recipient of the attribute of *al-Wakīl*. He evolves from a state in which he sees Allah's hand in the causes and reasons of things, to a state where all causes and reasons disappear. He fully gives his life into the hand of the ultimate Trustee, and in turn becomes His trusted servant. Allah's trusteeship is thereby manifested in him.

AL-QAWĪ

القوي جل جلاله

Allah is the Most Strong One, the Inexhaustible.

He possesses all strength. He is able to overcome all, and none may touch Him. On the action of His strength there are no conditions that are difficult or easy. He can create a billion universes with the same ease with which He creates a blade of grass. With His inexhaustible strength He sees to the continuation of the creation and the protection of the creatures, and guides their actions until the appointed time.

ʿAbd al-Qawī is the servant who is honored with the manifestation of the strength of *al-Qawī*. With Allah's power in him he defeats lust, worldly ambition, anger and negativity, and the other soldiers of the Devil. By the grace of the manifestation of that name in him he becomes able to destroy, always and everywhere, all enemies—man, devil, or jinn. None can oppose him. He repels all opponents through the power of Allah, whose strength is victorious over all.

AL-MATĪN

المتين جل جلاله

Allah is perfect in His strength and in His firmness.

The attribute of *al-Qawī* pertains to the perfection of His power, while the attribute of *al-Matīn* is the vehemence, the all-pervasive action of this strength. None can be saved from this strength; no force can oppose it. Nothing causes difficulty for it, nothing can weaken it, nor does that strength need any aid.

Allah has compassion and He has punishment. When He extends His compassion to His beloved servants, none can prevent this beneficence from reaching its destination, nor can any conceivable power prevent His vengeance, anger, and punishment from hitting its target. The servant should hope for all good and beauty to come from Allah, and should fear only Allah's punishment. Thus all other fears disappear from the hearts of servants who are attached to their Lord.

'Abd al-Matīn is the servant to whom the mystery of the attribute of the all-pervasive strength of Allah is given. That strength makes him hold to his religion with such strength and patience that nothing can tempt him away from it, no difficulty will tire him, and nothing can separate him from the Truth. In the defense of the Truth, no one can frighten him nor silence him. His effect is upon everything, and none other that Allah can affect him.

AL-WALĪ

الولي جل جلاله

Allah is the protecting friend of His good servants.

He helps His good servants; He eliminates their difficulties and gives them guidance, peace and success in their affairs in this world and in the Hereafter. He takes them out of darkness into light and enlightens their hearts; these hearts do not stay constricted and attached to the present, but stretch to times before the before and after the after. They come to know the Lord of these realms, acknowledge His unity and oneness, and are honored by the highest level that can be reached by mankind—His friendship—through being a good servant to him.

Allah's friends have eyes enlightened by and seeing with the divine light. They take lessons from all they hear and see. Divine light shines through their faces; whoever sees them remembers Allah. There is neither fear nor sadness for them, for they do not know any other friend but Allah. They fear nothing except opposing Allah's pleasure. They neither need nor expect anything from anyone except Allah.

Try to gain Allah's friendship. Be friends with His friends and learn to be like His friends. Believe in what they believe, do what they do, reject what they reject, love the ones they love, and above all, love the One whom they love most.

'Abd al-Walī is the servant in whom the friendship of everyone who is faithful becomes manifest; he is a friend to all those who are pure and devout believers.

الحميد جل جلاله

AL-ḤAMĪD

Allah is the Most Praiseworthy.

He is the one praised by all existence. Praising is honoring with respect and thankfulness the Great One who gives infinite gifts. All that exist praise Allah with their tongues, with their actions, or simply by their very existence. He is the only one who is worthy of devotion, of respect, of thankfulness, and of praise. How can one praise another than Him in His presence, while all is from Him? He is the source of all gifts and all perfection.

He has given us life, a beautiful form, strength, intelligence, language, and so forth, directly. He has given us gifts brought to us by the hands of other men or by the intermediary of His other creations. These gifts praise Allah; the ones through whose hands these gifts came praise Allah;

should we not praise Allah? Man invented the computer, which works, speaks, writes, communicates, captures the forms and sounds of things. The machine itself, in doing these things, praises its inventor. It is in this way that all nature praises Allah with its existence and its function. The people who use and benefit from that computer praise its inventor. That is how the servant praises the Creator. Then the inventor praises himself. Allah the Inventor of all this praises Himself and is not in need of the praise of any other.

Allah in His mercy and generosity has ordered man to perform certain duties for his own good, and to escape from certain evils for his own peace and salvation. There are such duties to be executed at every hour of one's life; when one performs these duties in their appointed times one receives both material benefit and spiritual joy and wisdom, especially if these tasks are done for Allah's sake. A reward of special enlightenment comes with it. Man learned what he knew with it, and man advanced with it. With what Allah forbade man to do, He protects him from Hellfire.

The greatest of all the sins is *kufr*, denial; denial is the opposite of praise. Imagine a benefactor of a community who has helped everyone, from whom everyone equally profited, and furthermore, on whom the life and harmony of that society depend. If someone insulted this benefactor, denied his good deeds, what would the community that loved and respected him do? They would all be angry, hostile, vengeful towards that person. Although that person had not done any harm to the people, all the people would hate him and curse him and try to destroy him. Because he had insulted the benefactor, the people would consider the harm done to all of them.

That is how, if one denies Allah's existence, or criticizes His canons, or minimizes His perfect qualities and beneficent doings, one is cursed not only by men, but by all creation. Since there is no place which is not His, such a one will not be able to escape. We take refuge from Him in Him. All praise is due to the Lord of the whole creation, who leads us from darkness to light, who clears hearts of the night of denial and fills them with the divine light of faith. *Al-ḥamdu lillāhi rabb il-'alamīn.*

'Abd al-Ḥamid is he to whom Allah shows Himself with His most beautiful attributes. All these beauties become manifest in him. Therefore all men praise him, but he praises only Allah.

المحصي جل جلاله

AL-MUḤSĪ

Allah is the possessor of all quantitative knowledge.

He sees and knows everything in its reality. In addition to knowing all existence as an inseparable whole, He knows each thing analytically separated according to its kind, its class; and as well as knowing it individually He knows its parts, even its atoms. He counts and calculates to the exact number. He knows the number of all existences in the created universe, though it seems infinite to us, down to the number of breaths exhaled and inhaled by each of His creatures. He counts and weighs, one by one, all our good deeds and sins, registering all in a great ledger.

As in His attributes *al-'Alīm*, the one who knows all that happens, *al-Khabīr*, the one who knows all inner occurrences, and *ash-Shahīd*, the one who witnesses all that there is, *al-Muḥsī*, the one who analyzes, counts and records in quantities, is an attribute that should encourage the friends of Allah who do right and admonish His enemies who do wrong. Even if a good deed or a sin is as small as a mustard seed, it is counted and not lost.

The good servant, aware of this attribute, should analyze in himself the thing that he intends to do, whether it is right or wrong. He should watch himself at every breath and be aware. He should make his accounting often, five times a day, at the time of each prayer, and be thankful to Allah for the good which came through him, assume the responsibility for his sins, and repent. Salvation is in making one's accounting now, well before the Day of Last Judgment, the terrible day of accounting before your Lord.

'Abd al-Muḥsī is he who is honored with the ability and will to count everything, to whom the quantity of all is made known. He not only knows things in width and depth around himself, but also knows his own acts and words and being analytically, and lives accordingly.

AL-MUBDĪ'

المُبْدِئُ جَلَّ جَلَالُه

Allah is the originator of all. He creates without model or material.

In the beginning before time or space, Allah existed. There was none other than He, none who could profit Him or hurt Him. There were no models of things to be, nor material to make them from. Allah Most High, to manifest His existence, to make known His beauty and perfection, and to make felt His love and compassion, created the creation and produced the first models. In order that the creation proliferate and continue, He made each original creation a means of perpetuating its own kind in accordance with causes, conditions, and canons of a divine order, which He also created.

Those who think of these means as the originators of things that exist, and think of nature as God, must contemplate what it is that moved the void; who charged the proton and the electron; what force it is that is inexhaustible, that sustains the continuity of things.

The servant inspired by this attribute must seek to understand his origins; how, from nothing, he and everything else came to be a creature that lives, grows, sees, hears, speaks, thinks—exquisite, in perfect order—and to confirm that none else but Allah, the originator of all creation, without the influence or help of anything, is responsible for it all. Anyone who thinks of a partner to Allah becomes guilty of the only unpardonable sin, attributing an equal to Allah, polytheism.

'Abd al-Mubdī' is the servant who receives the secret of the Originator, to whom Allah reveals the origin and the source of everything, and who becomes a witness to the beginning of everything.

AL-MU'ĪD المعيد جل جلاله

Allah is the restorer of the things that He has created and destroyed.

The attribute of *al-Mubdī'*, the Originator, contains the meaning of the Inventor, while *al-Mu'īd* is the Re-creator and the Restorer to previous form. Everything runs through its predestined period of life and passes away. Finally nothing exists except Allah, as it was in the beginning. Yet all the doings of the creation, especially of man, are recorded within the eternally existent and eternally alive Allah. Some lived according to His laws, pure and decent. Others claimed "freedom" and revolted, murderous and tyrannical. The law of man did not catch and punish one thousandth of them. Allah knows all; He is the Most Just; He does not love tyrants, and he takes vengeance against them. If all is resolved by death, there is no eternal justice. Then the sinner, the revolter, the tyrant, would escape punishment. Even human reason cannot accept this.

Without a doubt there will be a Day of Last Judgment, where the good and the evil will be separated from each other. The good will receive their reward, the bad their punishment. Allah promises this in His Qur'an, and Allah keeps His promises. On that day, Allah al-Mu'id will re-create all creatures, perfect to the details of their fingerprints, and return their souls to them.

The servant who is aware of this recognizes Him not only as his Creator, but as the one who will re-create him. He will be loyal to Him alone, and will not revolt against the Creator for the sake of the created.

'Abd al-Mu'īd is he within whom Allah has placed the knowledge of the secret that things are continuously being re-enacted. Often that servant helps in the re-creation of things and the recurrence of affairs. He helps to maintain the re-created and the recurrent.

AL-MUḤYĪ

المحيي جل جلاله

Allah is the giver of life to things without life.

As Allah can make that which does not exist come to be, as Allah can give life to the one without life, Allah can kill a thing and restore its life. Allah is the one who has created life and who has created death; none else can do that. Think of yourself. Once you were nonexistent, you were not alive. Allah created us in our mothers' wombs and gave us life, brought us to this world to breathe, to eat, to grow . . . . He gave us strength, the ability to think, to seek, to find, to know, to hear, to talk, to build, to destroy, and to propagate. All this, and this life, does not belong to us. It is a gift, lent to us. The only thing that is ours is the choice we make in the testing ground that this world and this life are: to believe or to disbelieve, to obey or to revolt—which will qualify us for heaven or hell when we will die and be brought back to life again.

The believer is thankful for the life he has received. This thankfulness is put into action by working hard for Allah's sake to serve His creatures continuously as if he is never going to die. One should also continuously remember death, and work for the Hereafter, for one's salvation, as if one is going to die at the next moment.

'Abd al-Muḥyī is he who brings his heart to life. A heart filled with the beasts of this world is dead. A heart that is cleansed of this world and contains none but Allah is alive, and is the house of Allah. To such a servant, Allah may even give permission, as He did for Jesus, (May Allah bless him), to restore the dead to life.

المميت جل جلاله

AL-MUMĪT

Allah is the creator of death.

All who are alive will certainly die. Death may come at any moment. Allah Most High has destined a time for each being to come into existence, and a time to leave.

Man is made of a combination of the flesh and the soul. The flesh is visible; the soul is hidden. The body is temporal; the soul is eternal. Thus there are two lives in man, the temporal and the eternal. The life of the material being starts with conception and ends in death, when the soul leaves the body. Although the soul continues to exist without the body, it has no physical feeling or movement, as if paralyzed. As the one who is totally paralyzed knows his state, so does the dead one know his state. Death is like a total paralysis, affecting the heart, the mind, the nerves, the circulation—everything.

In life, the body is under the orders of the soul. In death, the soul is like a king who has lost his kingdom. In life, the soul is like a merchant who buys and sells, profits and loses. In death, it is like a merchant who has lost his business; he cannot gain any more. He is left with whatever he has gained or whatever he has lost, his debts. In his grave, he waits—either bankrupt, hungry, cold, in pain, or in plenty, joy and peace—until the Day of Last Judgment.

The believer is not afraid of death; he prepares for it. Death is Allah's will. Whether you say that all is here, that there is nothing after this, or you believe that every day has a tomorrow and this world has a Hereafter, you will leave here sooner or later. If you seek the pleasures of this world alone, when this life ends, your happiness will end. All your work, all your plans, all your hopes will end. But if you profit from this world, perfecting your faith, acquiring wisdom, gathering its fruits and preparing for the Hereafter, when this short life is over you will find eternal bliss. Allah in His mercy and generosity gives what His servants ask for, regardless of faith or faithlessness. If you wish for this world, you will receive it. If you wish for the eternal life of the Hereafter, you will receive it.

'Abd al-Mumīt is he in whose heart lust, love of this world and negativity are killed by Allah. Thus this heart has found true life. When the negative forces of the ego in one's heart are dead, one is illuminated with the divine light. Such a light enlightens those around one also. Such a person continues living, breathing the air of a divine and eternal life.

AL-ḤAYY

الحي جل جلاله

Allah is the perfectly alive and ever-living one.

That which is alive is cognizant and active. Allah is cognizant of all, and all actions are His. All that is known and will be known is within His knowledge; all existence is always comprehended in His action.

With the exception of Allah, the life of all that is living is held within the limits of its action and its realization. That realization and activity are the signs of life. When these end, life ends. The value of each life is judged by the extent of the knowledge and the activity of the living one. Allah Most High has given lives of different degrees and different kinds to His Creation. The value of a created being is in accordance with the degree of the signs of life in it.

A plant, which is alive, is more valuable than soil or stone. Plants are born, eat, drink, grow, propagate, and die. They also possess knowledge, enabling them to differentiate that which is profitable from that which is harmful for them. They are also active. They seek and find what is needed for their growth and propagation in the air, in the water, and in the depths of the earth. They suck in what they need and they digest it and transform it into food, fruit, remedies, and thousands of things that are beneficial to higher forms of life. Yet they are unaware that there is a higher form of life than theirs.

Life in the animal is higher because the animal sees, hears, and moves. The life of vegetation is inferior to the life of the animal; that is why the animal is the master of vegetation. It steps on it, grazes and eats it. There is life superior to that of the animal. The Creator has honored man with that superiority.

The life of man contains all the qualities of vegetal and animal life, only in perfected form. In addition, he has intellect. This intellect with which he has been honored analyzes, compares, concludes, figures out the end at the beginning, and takes action in accordance. He knows and acts upon his knowledge; that is why he is the master of this world. The most elementary signs of life are birth, eating and drinking, breathing, growth and propagation. The higher sign of the higher form of life is to know and to act in accordance with that knowledge.

Men differ also in the degree of their aliveness, which is judged by the extent of their knowledge and their action. The lowest degree of knowledge for men is the awareness and knowledge of himself. He who does not know himself and is not aware of his existence may as well be dead. The words of unconscious dead men are dead and deadly; run away from them. Within the sacred name *Ḥayy*, pronounced by men of *ma'rifah* to whom the mystery of the Ever-Living One has been divulged, there is life. Hear it from their mouths and let it penetrate to your souls, so that you too may come alive.

'Abd al-Ḥayy is he in whom Allah has killed the worldly desires of his flesh, thus giving him the eternal life of knowing himself.

AL-QAYYŪM

الْقَيُّومُ جَلَّ جَلَالُهُ

Allah is the Ever Self-Existing One upon whom the existence of all depends.

His existence depends on none other than Himself. His existence is over all other existences. He is the one who gives that which is necessary for the existence of everything. He has created the causes for the existence of everything until the destined time. All exists because of Him.

If man can see how his being, his life, his body are dependent on his soul, he may understand a little bit the dependence of all that exists upon the Ever Self-Existent One. The soul governs the whole being of man. When the soul leaves the body, although the body appears the same, it does not breathe, it does not see, it does not hear, it does not move, and eventually it disintegrates, because what governed it and held it together was the soul.

It is the soul which is reponsible for life, existence, and order and harmony within the whole being. The being—its wisdom, its beauty, its strength, its very life down to the last cell, the last atom—is in need of the soul at every moment.

When the soul leaves, all these qualities disappear.

Like this, every atom of the created universe at every moment is in need of the divine favor, the manifestation of *al-Qayyūm*. This divine grace is a special will of Allah that is present always, in different forms and strengths, in accordance with the need of everything in the universe for the perpetuation and amelioration it alone grants. It is with that divine will that every atom obtains the cause for the satisfaction of its needs. If Allah cut off that favor for a split second, none would be left on their feet.

O heedless one, Allah, who has infinite numbers of good servants and the whole creation to take care of, nevertheless cares for you and maintains you as if you were His only creation. Although you have no one else but Him who keeps you, you behave as if you do not need Him and have other protectors who could care for you. Worse still, you behave as if you are self-sufficient, self-existent. How great is Allah's favor, how infinite is His mercy, and how deep is your heedlessness!

'Abd al-Qayyūm is he who witnesses that all exists because of Allah, and becomes an instrument of the manifestation of *al-Qayyūm* by meeting the needs of others in Allah's name.

الواجد جل جلاله

AL-WĀJID

Allah finds and obtains whatever He wishes whenever He wishes.

Allah is able to find any of His creation instantly, especially when He wishes to exercise His will upon it. It is even superfluous to use the word "find," because all is in His presence at all times. None can hide or retreat to a place that is out of His reach. Allah has all He needs to exercise His will. The servant must never consider himself separated from his

Lord. His Lord is ever-present within and without him, and the servant is ever in the presence of his Lord. When the servant has a need, it suffices him to feel and say, "O Lord, I am in Your presence and my state and my needs are better known to You than to myself."

One is always in need. There is always trouble for which one seeks relief. At times, one feels the need of others like oneself—a doctor, a lawyer, a judge. It is not possible to seek an audience with these people at any time of the day or night; such ceremony and difficulty one must go through to present one's case to them! Yet how often we have to go through that while the Lord of all these servants, the Curer, the just Judge, the rich Sustainer, the Merciful, the Best of Masters, the Loving One, the All-Powerful, the Ever-Present, invites us to His presence five times a day, at the appointed times of prayer, and we neglect to go to Him to present our needs! Not only five times a day, but wherever you are, at whatever time of the day or night, He is there to satisfy your needs with all His love and compassion and wisdom and treasure. All you need to say is *Yā Allāh*.

'Abd al-Wājid is he who finds everything in the essence of the One. He knows the place of everything and is able to find it. Because he can obtain everything he wishes, he neither loses nor asks for anything. He finds that which Allah wishes him to find.

AL-MĀJID

الماجد جل جلاله

Allah is the Most Glorious, who shows infinite generosity and munificence to those close to Him.

For example, He gives them the gift of good character and good conduct, enabling them to do good deeds; then He glorifies them for the character He has given, and rewards them by forgiving their sins and their errors. He hides their sins and errors from others and even from themselves. He accepts their excuses; He protects their rights. He relieves their difficulties. He prepares the causes for their peace, happiness, and salvation. The servant, remembering the munificence of the Glorious One, should love Him and obey His orders with joy, and fear Him through loving Him, fearing to lose the favor of the Beloved One.

'Abd al-Mājid is he who is praised and honored by Allah and given the strength to carry the responsibility of this honor.

الواحد جل جلاله

AL-WĀḤID

Allah is One. He has no equal, none like Him, nor any partner in His essence, in His attributes, in His actions, in His orders, or in His beautiful names.

He is One in His essence. All else is His creation. How could any of what He has made and maintained be compared to Him?

He is One in His attributes. Among His creation, and especially in man, there may be signs or symbols of His attributes in order that we feel a sense of His qualities and strengthen our faith; otherwise the manifestations of His attributes are not like His attributes at all.

He is One in His actions. He does not need any help in His act of creation, nor in doing what He wills with His creation. What appear as material and spiritual causes to us are unable to cause anything by themselves.

He is One in His orders and in His justice. He is the only source of reward, punishment, good deeds or sin. None other than He has the right to say "This is right, this is wrong, this is lawful, this is unlawful."

He is One in His beautiful names, none of which can be attributed to other than Him. Anyone who in any way seeks the resemblance of anything to Him is guilty of the only unforgiveable sin—to attribute partners to Him. He is the only one worthy of worship. His oneness is indivisible. He is a whole without parts.

In man, the sign of the Oneness is manifested in the one who has reached such a height in good morals, character, and manners that there is no other man so excellent as he. Yet the uniqueness of this man is limited by the span of his lifetime. Others like him could have existed before, or will exist after him. His uniqueness is only in relation to the aspect of character and does not include all possible considerations.

'Abd al-Wāḥid is he who has penetrated into the oneness of his Lord and who has come to know the mystery of this attribute, which becomes the key to the understanding of all the attributes of Allah, so that he sees everything within the beautiful names. He understands everything through the attributes of Allah and does everything in accordance with them. He is the master of the age. He is the first of his time after Allah. He is the *quṭb*.

AṢ-ṢAMAD

الصَّمَدُ جَلَّ جَلَالُهُ

Allah is the satisfier of all needs, and all is in need of Him.

He is the sole recourse, the only place of support where one may go to rid oneself of all trouble and pain and to receive all that one needs through the blessings of this name. Inexhaustible treasures open and are distributed to all creatures in accordance with their needs.

There are men and other creatures of Allah who serve as sources from whom one seeks cure for one's troubles and satisfaction of one's needs. However, as the needs are different, the sources corresponding to these needs differ. If one needs wisdom, one seeks a man of knowledge. If one needs money, one goes to someone rich. If one is sick, one finds a doctor. It is not always certain that the scholar is going to answer your question, nor that the rich one will pay the money you need, nor that the doctor will be able to cure you; and they are not so readily available. One must go to them and wait for them to have time for you. These sources are the signs, the reflections of the attribute *aṣ-Ṣamad*, and indeed are a great gift from Allah.

The Satisfier of all needs is ever-present, knowing your needs before you do, satisfying your needs in the way they should be satisfied, not in the way you think they should be satisfied. It is good that you realize your need, that you ask for its satisfaction and that you accept and are thankful for whatever manner it is in which He sees fit to satisfy it. It is good only to make you aware of your Creator and to make you aware of yourself. Otherwise, strictly for the satisfaction of the need, neither your having it nor asking for its satisfaction, nor your being cognizant of having received the satisfaction, are necessary. For Allah is the All-Knowing, All-Powerful, Generous, Compassionate Satisfier of all needs.

However, He loves His servants who are heedful more than those who are heedless. He loves His servants who are thankful more than those who are thankless.

'Abd aṣ-Ṣamad has received from Allah the duty of the maintenance and education of His creation. His hand, his tongue, his whole being are a means through which Allah satisfies the needs of the creation. That is why all seek him for the elimination of their troubles, for receiving good, for acceptance of their repentance, to escape from God's anger. He is the intercessor.

Allah Al Qādir, Al-Muqtadir, Al-Muqaddim

۳۰ AL-QĀDIR القَادِرُ جَلَّ جَلَالُهُ

Allah is the All-Powerful who does what He wills the way He wills.

Allah has created the universe as a mirror to reflect His power. He created the universe by Himself, without needing the help of anything, from nothing, with neither materials nor model. He said "Be!" and it became. If He wills, He can destroy everything and send all back to nothingness. If a thing has not happened, it is not because He has not the power to make it happen, it is because He has not willed it.

Al-Qādir has infinite ability. His possibility of causing things to happen, His power of invention and creation are only conditioned by one thing: His will.

What befits the good servant of Allah is to look at that mirror He has created to reflect His power and to see the billions of suns and galaxies within the immeasurable depths of the heavens above, defying mind and imagination. He should observe also how, just as these galaxies swim in their allotted paths, innumerable cratures swim in a drop of water under a microscope; how from two cells He creates a human being who becomes a microcosm containing all that exists in the universe; how He gives a tiny piece of bone in the ear the ability to hear and a piece of meat in the mouth the ability to speak. Isn't the believer going to prostrate himself in awe and respect? This is his greatest honor.

'Abd al-Qādir is he who is a witness to everything made by the Hand of Power of Allah. The manifestation of Allah's power is spoken of as "Allah's hand." Nothing can stop that which is made by Allah's hand.

AL-MUQTADIR

المقتدر جل جلاله

Allah is the one who creates all power and has total control over all power.

Because He has total power, He is able to create what He wills and put in His creation whatever power He wills. Without this energy that comes from its Creator, everything in itself is lacking, unable, in need; but if Allah gives it the power and enables it, an ant can move a mountain. Allah bestows power upon things on earth and in heaven, and uses them in accordance with His all-pervasive wisdom and will. If He wills, He strengthens the weak and weakens the strong, makes peace beween them, makes them love each other; or if He wills, He makes them fight each other.

Allah is the helper of the well-intentioned who serve for His sake; Allah is the enemy of tyrants. He gives ease, wisdom, patience, perseverance and strength to His good servants. He increases the heedlessness, ambition, pleasures and self-confidence of the tyrants. Allah manifests His name *al-Muqtadir*, along with *al-Qahhār*, the one supreme over all forces, and *al-Shadīd*, the one who is severe in punishment, who destroys His enemies, in defense of the righteous.

All creation is allotted a certain power by *al-Muqtadir*. These powers are limited and controlled by the Giver of power. It seems to us that the powers of man are great, enabling him to do great deeds. We even say that he can invent, he can create. Man can neither invent nor create. Allah causes a thing to happen and leads man to discover something that has already been created. It is always Allah who creates, even if sometimes it appears to come about through His creatures.

The believer should know that all power comes from *al-Muqtadir*, and by submission to His will, by obeying Him, by loving and fearing Him, one should try to obtain that power. No force can overcome that power. All love the one who loves Allah; all fear the one who fears Allah.

When one receives the help of Allah and is victorious through it, one should not be spoiled and become self-confident. On the contrary, one should show one's thankfulness actively by repenting for one's mistakes, by being just, forgiving, generous, and compassionate, even to one's enemies.

'Abd al-Muqtadir is he upon whom Allah has bestowed the knowledge of the secret of His first act of creation, the creation of the causal primary intelligence, *an-nūr al-Muḥammadī*, from which all other created existence was generated.

AL-MUQADDIM

المقدم جل جلاله

Allah brings forward whomever He wills.

Allah advances the chosen among His creation, bringing some above and ahead of others. For instance, Allah invites the whole of humanity to truth, but leads some to respond to this invitation, while others are left behind. Allah creates all human beings as Muslims; some realize their Islam, their submission, while others are left behind. Allah has made things lawful and unlawful for all men. To some, he has given discrimination; these abide by His law and advance. Others are trampled upon.

Allah favors some of his servants by the quiet love He creates in the hearts of people for them, and others by loud cheers and applause. There are great kings whose deaths were celebrated by their people with joy. There are poor men whose departures the world mourned.

The believer knows that although Allah is the one who advances whom He wills, He has also set laws of action for us. If we do not do anything and we are lazy, the end is poverty, constriction, trouble and pain. If we work for money and fame, that money will be spent on drinking, gambling, debauchery. The end of that will again be poverty, constriction and pain.

Man must be in harmony with Allah al-Muqaddim, work in accordance with His laws to advance. If the goal is to obtain the good of this world in a lawful manner, and if Allah does not permit the servant to become rich, although he tries very hard, still Allah knows best. Perhaps such acceptance is a greater advancement than being ahead in riches. For the measure of true advancement is the degree of one's closeness to Allah.

'Abd al-Muqaddim is he whom Allah keeps in the first rank in every respect. Allah also gives him control over the ones who are going to advance and the ones who have moved ahead.

AL-MU'AKHKHIR المؤخر جل جلاله

Allah is He who leaves whomever He wills behind, and delays advancement.

As He leads some into advancement, He leads others into regression. As He rewards some whose efforts are in harmony with His will by bringing them to the first rank, He leaves others behind who are making the same effort. There is always a reason. If a believer is left behind in spite of his efforts, there may be some wrong, some impurity, some hypocrisy in his intentions. Or it may be that advancement for him should necessitate more difficulty and pain so that he will value the reward more and better guard his station when he reaches it.

Advancement and being left behind are also relative. The one in the first rank surely is ahead, but the one in the second rank, although behind the first, is ahead of the third. Allah in His wisdom advances and keeps back whomever He wills. The good servant accepts his station and state, continuing his efforts but also trying to understand the reasons for his state.

The good servant should know that what is most important is his closeness to Allah. The means of closeness to Him are *'ibādah* and *'ubūdiyyah*. *'Ibādah* is to do things to please Allah and *'ubūdiyyah* is to be pleased with what Allah does.

'Abd al-Mu'akhkhir is he who becomes instrumental in postponing the punishment of the ones who revolt against the *sharī'ah*, who go astray, who tyrannize themselves and others. He also becomes an instrument to stop these sinners at a certain point.

AL-AWWAL

الأوّل جلّ جلاله

Allah is the First.

Even when we say He is before the before, the first "before" is before the second and in comparison with it. His being first is not even related to that which comes after Him—which is all existence, seen and unseen—because that would mean that while He is the First, there is still a second. There is none like Him. His firstness means that there is none prior to Him, that He is self-existent, that all comes from Him and that He is the cause of all that became. By the grace of this attribute, the good servant should be the first in devotion, worship, and good deeds.

'Abd al-Awwal is the servant who has been given the secret of the beginnng and the end of everything. He is aware of eternity and endlessness.

Allāh Muqaddim, Ya Mu'akhkhir, Ya Awwal, Ya Ākhir, Ya Ẓāhir

AL-ĀKHIR

الآخِرُ جَلَّ جَلَالُهُ

Allah is the Last.

We cannot say that He is after the after, because He cannot be compared to that which would then precede Him. As He has no beginning, He has no end. He is eternal. All existence has two ends: a beginning when it is created, born; and an end when it dies and disappears.

He is before the before because He has created the first existence from nothing; He is the Last because when all disappears only He will exist.

> Everyone on it passes away and there endures forever the person of thy Lord, the Lord of Glory and Honor.
>
> Surah Rahman (26-7)

All existence will return to Him. He is the Last in the sense that the circle of existence begins and ends with Him. The beginning and the end of all is from Him, all comes from Him and all goes to Him. There is nothing before Him and there is nothing after Him.

The believer knows that all he has, material and spiritual, is His and will return to Him. He himself will return to Him and will have to give an accounting of how he used and cared for that which was lent to him temporarily. Therefore the actions of the good servant from beginning to end are performed for His sake, for His good pleasure, and in the name of good servantship.

It is proper to read, to recite and to consider the attributes "The First" and "The Last" together, because the meaning is like a circle where the first and the last are one.

'Abd al-Ākhir is he who knows that everything has an end except Allah Most High, who is the only Eternal One. He works to lose his temporal self in the eternalness of his Lord.

AẒ-ẒĀHIR

الظاهر جل جلاله

Allah is the Manifest One.

A thing is apparent to some and hidden from others in accordance with their abilities to see and to realize. Allah Most High is hidden from those who seek to see by means of their senses or their imagination, but He is apparent to those who seek to know Him by the inference of that treasure of wisdom and reason that Allah has bestowed upon them.

Allah is hidden in the endlessness of His infinite power and existence. He is like a light that makes all visible, yet His Light itself becomes a veil to His Light. That which has no bounds seems not to have a shape, therefore becoming invisible. But He is apparent in everything: everything our eyes see, every sound we hear, everything we touch, everything we taste. The meaning of everything we think, everything without and everything within us, is not Him but is from Him. Everything is a proof of His existence. Everything says, "I am nothing on my own. The one who made me, who keeps and maintains me, is my Creator. I am in need of Him every moment of my existence. Every shape, every color, every taste, every perfume, every movement, every force, every quality that appears in me is from Him. It is His making, His gift, His bounty, His work."

Allah is manifest in His attributes. One can know an artist from his artwork. If one does not see the setting sun, but sees its reflection in distant windows and says that he has seen the sunset, he is not lying. If one sees the perfect attributes of Allah in His creation, within and without himself, and says, "I have seen Allah," he is not lying.

One is able to see only what is closest to one, and that which is closest to you is yourself. Man is Allah's best creation. All creation is within man. If you see His perfect attributes in the perfect creation that you are, you will see Allah the Manifest One, and your faith will be complete.

The apparent and the hidden are also in man. His form, his words, his actions, and his work are manifest. His feelings and thoughts are hidden. Man is not what he is only because of what is manifest in him. He may grow fat or thin, he may even lose a limb—but his essence, his identity, that which is he, that which is constant, is hidden in him. His identity becomes manifest only through his action, through the evaluation of the quality of his actions.

'Abd aẓ-Ẓāhir is the one to whom the inner meaning of things becomes outwardly manifest, like the prophet Moses (May Allah bless him), upon whom the secret of the Manifest One was bestowed. He saw the manifestation of the divine light in the flames of the Burning Bush, and invited the Bani Israel to faith with a huge Torah revealed to him in golden script, ordering worldly law, salvation from the hand of the tyrant, and the benefits of Paradise.

AL-BĀṬIN

الْبَاطِنُ جَلَّ جَلَالُهُ

Allah is the Hidden One.

His existence is both manifest and hidden. He is apparent because the signs of His existence are even visible to the blind, but His essence is hidden from us. If there is an artwork, there certainly is an artist who has created that artwork. If there is a creation, there certainly is a Creator. If you exist, He exists. But to truly know the Creator is not possible for the creature because the knowledge, the mind, the understanding of the created one are limited. Therefore they encompass only a limited area. Allah Most High is eternal, infinite, without a beginning or an end, inexhaustible in His knowledge and power. To expect a temporal, limited existence to understand and encompass an eternal and infinite concept is absurd. Is it possible to fit an ocean into a bucket? Yet although a bucketful of water from the ocean is not the ocean, it is *from* the ocean. The manifestation of His attributes in His creation is like that bucket of water: not Him, but from Him. His hidden essence is like the ocean whose depths and width are infinite, unfathomable.

To know the essence of anything, no matter how small—to know it in totality, outwardly and inwardly, to penetrate all its secrets—is practically impossible. Science in its advanced state today, and in what we imagine it will become tomorrow, always ends and always will end in impotence and awe. Of everything in creation, we are closest to ourselves. Has man been able to know and understand himself?

That is why the Messenger of Allah (Peace and Blessings of Allah be upon him) ordered us to contemplate Allah in His attributes and forbade us to think further than that. Only Allah knows His own essence; we have no power to conceive of it. Those who pushed their minds to go further either lost their wits or fell into the chasm of disbelief, faithlessness, and attributing partners to Allah.

'Abd al-Bāṭin is the good servant upon whom Allah bestows the knowledge of his heart, whose inner self is purified, whose spirituality surpasses his material being, for whom the veils part, the secrets become manifest, the future known. He becomes an instrument inviting men to cleanse their inner world with the divine light, and to reach spiritual perfection. Allah, the Hidden One, manifested His attribute *al-Bāṭin* in the prophet Adam (May Allah bless him), and taught him not only the manifestation of His attributes but the meaning of them as well. Until Adam (May Allah bless him), even the angels knew Allah through the manifestation of His attributes. That is the difference between Adam (May Allah bless him) and the angels in the degree of perfection of faith. That is why Allah ordered the angels to prostrate themselves in front of Adam (May Allah bless him), and that is why Adam (May Allah bless him) became the teacher of the angels.

AL-WĀLI

الْوَالِى جَلَّ جَلَالُهُ

Allah is the sole Manager and Governor of the whole creation.

His government is of such might that the whole creation from beginning to end (even before its creation!) is under its will and power. With the single order "Be!" it came into existence from nonexistence. All appears in this way: managed, developed, and when its time comes, dying, disappearing from sight. Even after death, everything stays under His government, and finally will be brought back to life again. In His managing of the creation, Allah knows at all times what has happened, what is happening, and what will happen, as all is planned, predestined. He is the one who wills and He is the one who executes.

Prior to your creation, He prepared a program for you: at what moment and place and from which mother you would be born, and all that would happen to you, all that you would do every minute of your life, up to the number of breaths you would inhale, up to the morsels of food that you would consume. Every syllable you will pronounce, every sound you will hear, all that you will see and all that you will do, is planned.

In the whole of creation, He has given will only to man. You think you can change your destiny with this will. In reality, it only serves your realizing, receiving, benefiting from, and enjoying that which is written for you. When you think you revolt, what would have happened to you still happens to you, only you are unaware, unconscious, resentful and in disharmony with that which is happening to you. Your will is your ability either to open your eyes—to see the creation of Allah in which His beautiful names are manifested, and to receive the light of faith and knowledge—or to revolt and sin, closing your eyes and remaining in darkness. Yet that which exists still exists, whether you see it or you are blind to it.

The whole of creation is governed by Allah's knowledge and power; not a leaf moves without His will. Neither is the movement of the leaf disconnected from other things moved by the same wind, by the same will.

Do not think you are left on your own. Know and see that you are part of a divine order under a just, compassionate, beneficent Governor. All is measured, all is registered, all moves swiftly. Use your will to be aware of it, to have faith in it and to be in harmony with it.

'Abd al-Wāli is he who governs himself and those who are entrusted to his care according to Allah's rules. He is just, he is good, and he dispenses justice and good. In return for his services he receives bounties and wisdom from Allah with which he further perfects his management and his generosity to other people.

As he teaches others to be just and generous like him, each time those he teaches act justly and generously, he receives twice the rewards they receive. The good ruler is the one whose good deeds will surpass his wrongdoings on the scale of the Day of Judgment. Allah keeps him under the shade of His throne. Allah is the helper of the one who helps others.

AL-MUTA'ĀLI

المتعالي جل جلاله

Allah is the Supreme One.

His greatness grows. As He gives from His inexhaustible treasures, His riches increase. As the needs of His creation increase, His bounties increase. Yet if all the forces, the conniving minds, and the armies of the entire universe united, they could not by force take anything from Him, even a thing the size of a mustard seed, without His permission and His will.

You might be strong, young and handsome today; you

may be sick, decrepit and crippled tomorrow. You might be wise and intelligent, but you may lose your wits tomorrow. You might be rich and become bankrupt. Think of the nations that were supreme on the face of this earth, but then were trampled and dishonored and have disappeared from the maps.

Allah the Supreme One is exempt from all such failures and defects.

The true servant, who sincerely says *amintu billāhi,* "I believe in Allah," believes in Him whose attributes, qualities, and beautiful names are described in the Holy Qur'an and the hadiths. There are also those who believe in nothing other than themselves, in this world, and in the joys, pleasures, and riches of this world. There are yet others who believe in gods who walk in the gardens of Eden in the cool of the day or walk upon the clouds or sit on thrones, who have wives and children, who regret having created some among their creations and some among men.

Allah the Supreme One is free from such attributions. Those who lower Him to the level of their imagination are lowering themselves from the high state of servantship to the lowest state of their evil-commanding egos.

'Abd al-Muta'āli is that exalted servant of Allah who climbs from one height to another in the comprehension of things within and without himself. He witnesses limitless divine heights, soaring to this level through Allah's generosity and reward for his continuous consciousness, remembrance and devotion. His whole purpose, intention, effort, and attention are focussed on knowing, finding, and being with Allah.

Allah Most High, in Surah Ta Ha, v. 114, addressing Muhammad (Peace and Blessings of Allah be upon him), the highest being in the entire creation, says:

> . . . (O My beloved) say: My Lord, increase me in knowledge.

Even he is ordered to wish to know more about his Lord.

AL-BARR البر جل جلاله

Allah is the perfect Doer of Good.

All good and bounty come from Him. He loves for His servants only good, comfort and ease. He does not like hardships for them, neither does He like those who create hardships. Yet in His mercy He forgives the ones who do no good. He hides meanness. If, in His justice, He chooses to punish, His punishment never exceeds the sin committed, while His reward for good deeds is tenfold. He delays His punishments so that perhaps the erring servant will realize his wrongdoing and repair it with a good deed. Then He transforms the sin that has been repented for into a good deed. If His servant intends to do a good deed but is unable to actualize it, He rewards the intention as if it were actualized. But if His servant intends to sin, and is unable to actualize it, He forgives him.

When you do good to Allah's creation, even if it is by a kind word or a smile, you see the reflection of Allah, the Perfect Doer of Good, in you. When the prophet Moses (May Allah bless him) talked to his Lord on Mount Sinai, he saw a man standing on the highest point of Allah's throne. He asked, "O Lord, how did this servant reach such heights?" Allah Most High answered, "He was never envious of the good that I bestowed upon my servants, and he was especially good to his mother and to his father." Those are the signs of Allah's goodness reflected upon His servant.

'Abd al-Barr is he in whom all the qualities of good, both material and spiritual, are manifest. Allah has given the possibility of wishing to do good to all believers. It becomes active in the one who submerges himself in the sea of mystery of Allah's beautiful name *al-Barr*.

AT-TAWWĀB

التَّوَّابُ جَلَّ جَلَالُهُ

Allah is He who constantly turns man to repentance.

Tawbah means to return: to return from revolt and sin to the straight path of virtue. Allah awakens the hearts of believers from the sleep of heedlessness through love of Him, with the manifestation of His existence around them, with the words of good advice of those who are close to Him, with the promise of His rewards and Paradise, and with the fear of His punishment and Hellfire.

Allah has servants whose hearts catch fire with a single spark. He also has servants whose hearts have turned to cold stone. If one poured heaps of fire upon them, they would still not become warm. Some have hearts like iron, which softens a bit from the fire and turns immediately back into iron again. That is why one has to be awakened frequently by listening to Allah's commands in the Qur'an. The whole universe—everything, including you—is the Qur'an. If you take lessons from what you see, within and outside yourself, you will wake up and return from the sinful state of unconsciousness and disharmony to the state of being in harmony with Allah's will. That is repentance acceptable to Allah, with which His anger is transformed into mercy, compassion and love.

The repentance that is acceptable to Allah is not simply seeing the wrong and ugliness of one's actions, regretting having done bad things and wishing not to repeat them, fearing Allah's punishment and hoping for Allah's mercy. This is like cutting off the crabgrass and leaving the root. One has to dig out all the roots. The repentance acceptable to Allah is the effort of inner cleaning, trying to eliminate the cause of the sins. Allah promises not only His mercy and forgiveness, but His love, to such purified ones.

When you are able to forgive and keep forgiving those who hurt you, you will see the manifestation of *at-Tawwāb* in yourself. Allah forgives the ones who forgive others. No matter how sinful they are, nor how often they forget their repentance, they must never doubt the mercy of Allah and the acceptance of their repentance.

'Abd at-Tawwāb is the blessed servant who has been made to return from the desires of his flesh and from the lies and imagination of this world to the Truth. By repeated repentance for his wrongdoings he has come to know the multiplicity in himself, and shedding it with his repentance, has achieved unity and oneness.

AL-MUNTAQIM

المنتقم جل جلاله

Allah is the Great Avenger.

Allah punishes those who persist in revolting, raving in their unconsciousness and egotism, creating disharmony, tyrannizing Allah's servants and His creation—these are the ones who are faithless and attribute partners to Allah. He gives them time and occasions to realize and repent for their wrongdoing. He warns them with repeated warnings. He accepts their excuses; He delays their punishment. In forgiving them, in delaying their punishment, His revenge becomes more terrible. For the persistent sinner has had further chances to sin, thus making himself deserving of harder punishment. Those who become the servants of their egos instead of becoming Allah's servants risk a terrible fall when they feel they are not punished for what they are doing. They are spoiled by Allah's mercy, soaring higher and higher in their arrogance. Suddenly, one day, Allah brings them down. The fall becomes greater from such heights. Many tyrants were brought to such heights before they were smashed. Allah makes those upon whom He takes vengeance a lesson to those whom He wishes to save.

Those who know how to take revenge upon the enemies of Allah, the greatest being their own egos, reflect Allah's attribute *al-Muntaqim*. Hz. Bayazid al-Bistami says, "One night I felt too tired and lazy to perform some of my devotions. I punished myself by not drinking water for a whole year."

'Abd al-Muntaqim is he whose vengeance upon the enemies of Allah is terrible, and who is most vengeful toward his own ego, which is his greatest enemy.

AL-'AFŪ العفو جل جلاله

Allah is the Forgiver, the Eliminator of sins.

Al-'Afū is the opposite of *al-Muntaqim*, the Avenger. Its meaning is close to that of *al-Ghafūr*, the All-Forgiving One, only it is more intensive. The root of the word *Ghafūr* means to overlook sins, while the root of the word *'Afū* means to destroy, eliminate sins. In the first instance the overlooked sins still exist; in the second, the eliminated sins disappear.

Allah loves to forgive, to erase sins. He does not often punish the ones who deny, the ones who revolt. He accepts their recognition of their sins as repentance. He erases their sins. Instead of punishment, He bestows His bounties upon them.

There is a secret in His delaying punishment and forgiving sins. In teaching us that Hellfire is there, He is teaching us that there are ways to salvation. It is like an announcement by a rich, generous, compassionate being, declaring: Our doors are open, our tables set. The one who accepts this invitation is welcome, and we do not reproach those who do not come to our feast.

Allah's bounties in this world, which are temporal, are

nothing in comparison to those promised in Paradise. The forgiving of sins is an encouragment to the deniers to change their ways, to come to the straight path, to Paradise. Allah's infinite mercy is certainly more than the sins of His servants. His doors are always open to the ones who choose to enter.

But those who are blind and deaf to the warning that is the compassion, mercy, and forgiveness of Allah, who persist in their infidelity and denial, who find justification for their denial in their being repeatedly forgiven, who are spoiled, who take pleasure in sinning, who try to lead others astray—they will finally be punished in this world by drowning in the gold they have accumulated, and in the Hereafter by Hellfire. That punishment does not negate the attribute of the Forgiving One, the Eliminator of sins, but it is a manifestation of His beautiful name the Just. Good and bad are not the same. If it were made to appear so, it might cause confusion in the mind of the good servant.

'Abd al-'Afū is the one who truly believes, who fears Allah—not so much Allah's punishment, but the loss of Allah's love. He is the one who has conscience, who has shame. And for him, the good and the bad that come to him from Allah are equal. He reflects the attribute *al-'Afū* by forgiving the one who tyrannizes him, by feeding the one who causes him hunger, by giving to the one who forcibly takes from him. Allah treats His servants the way they treat others.

AR-RA'ŪF

الرَّؤُوفُ جَلَّ جَلَالُهُ

Allah is All-Clement.

He has created all with His hand of power, and He can extinguish all, for He is not in need of His creation. This power and independence, His ability to see all, including the revolt and denial in some of His creation, does not prevent Him from His infinite mercy and clemency. On the contrary, in spite of His ability to see our sins, of His being just, of His being able to punish, the fact that He chooses to forgive proves His infinite mercy and clemency.

Even if one lacks faith and one's arrogance is boundless, even if one believes that one obtains one's livelihood by oneself and is the master of one's own destiny, look at the animals and plants—they are deaf, dumb, and mindless. How do they care for their offspring? How do birds build nests? Why are they not excessive in any direction that might cause their destruction, while man is? What is the mystery in that factory which is the silkworm, which builds its cocoon and produces the most beautiful and soft clothing, or the little bee who builds her hive and produces the sweetest of all foods?

These and all else are the signs of the clemency, mercy, and generosity around you. But for man, the manifestation of Allah's clemency is greater. He has " . . . created all and everything for you and you for Himself." He created you as the best of creation, perfect, as His deputy—to govern, to guide, to use His kingdom. He has given you the means to think, to talk, to read and write. He has taught you what is best for you, what is bad for you, the right and the wrong, the lawful and the unlawful. If you try to count His bounties and blessings upon you, you will be unable. For the believer and unbeliever alike, His generosity, mercy, and clemency are boundless.

The one in whom the clemency of Allah is reflected is the one who remembers his sins and realizes these bounties of Allah come in spite of his sins; he tries to serve Allah's creation with his mind, his body, and his property.

'Abd ar-Ra'ūf is he in whom Allah's mercy and compassion are manifest. He is clement in every way except regarding punishment in accordance with the *sharī'ah*. Although the justice of the religious law seems to be punishment, in reality it is mercy, because the fault for which one has paid is eliminated.

MĀLIK AL-MULK مَالِكُ الْمُلْك جَلَّ جَلَالُهُ

Allah is the eternal owner of His kingdom.

He shares neither the ownership nor the power, government, or guardianship of the universe with anyone. Indeed, the whole universe is one kingdom because all creation is interconnected—like man himself, whose hands, feet, eyes, mind, heart, and all organs are individual units, yet connected, forming a single totality.

The universe is a whole with harmonious parts, created for a purpose, realizing and fulfilling this purpose. Allah says, "I was a hidden treasure, I wished to be known; therefore I created the creation." Then the purpose and function of the creation is to know, to find, and to be with the Creator.

Man is the universe in microcosm; whatever exists in it exists in him. He is also the supreme creation and the deputy of Allah. That is why Allah bestows upon some of His servants, for a prescribed time, kingdoms, land, property, wealth; and lets them rule over them. Allah also gives them the knowledge of how to govern so that their kingdoms grow, their profits grow. He forbids them to follow their egos, their selfishness, which can only lead them to bankruptcy and perdition. If they become servants of their egos and use the wealth left in their care for themselves, all will be lost upon their deaths. They will be bankrupt, imprisoned in the dungeons of Hell. If men apply Allah's law to His kingdom which is lent to them and apply it to themselves as well, and if they govern for His pleasure and spend for His sake, the true Owner of the Kingdom will exchange the temporal kingdom He has bestowed upon them here for the eternal kingdom of the Hereafter.

ʿAbd Mālik al-Mulk becomes a witness of Allah's power over His kingdom. He therefore realizes that Allah uses him as His deputy in governing the universe and himself. This realization makes him a perfect servant, with Allah's rewards increasing to the greatest worldly heights. He depends on nothing except Allah, knowing that He is the only true King, and himself tries only to be a true servant—the highest level any human being can hope to reach.

DHŪL-JALĀLI WAL-IKRĀM ذُو الْجَلَالِ وَالْإِكْرَامِ

Allah is Lord of Majesty and Bounty.

There is no perfection that does not belong to Him, nor any blessing or honor that comes from other than Him. Allah is the owner of all majesty. Nothing else can even exist by itself, nothing can sustain itself. In His majesty, just as He created everything instantly, He can destroy it all instantly. On what power are you depending when you revolt against Him? To show His generosity, He has bestowed His bounty and honor upon you. Do not attribute this to yourself and glorify yourself. The honor He gave you is to make you see the Giver of the honor, the truly Honorable One. All is in need of Him; all comes from Him. Yet to tie every man to other men, to tie every creation to the rest of creation, Allah uses an invisible rope called need. He uses each man, each creation, as a means, as a vehicle to give to another what it needs. One must be grateful to the vehicle through which Allah's blessing comes, but one must know the true source and not forget to give all thanks to Him. All thanks are due to Him who not only sends us our worldly needs, but who has also promised us and taught us how to obtain His eternal blessings. These we can obtain by spending upon others, for His sake, that which He gave us through others' hands.

The Lord of Majesty and Bounty is one of those beautiful names that cannot be attributed to any but Allah. The ones who know have even claimed it to be *al-ism al-a'ẓam*, the greatest name of Allah.

'Abd Dhūl-Jalāli wal-Ikrām is he who fears only Allah, bows his head only to Him, and hopes to receive only from Him. This is the sign of the true believer's faith in the oneness of Allah. He expects nothing from men, neither does he fear their condemnation. For him, a sword held to his throat is no different from gold poured at his feet. He is neither worried by the one nor overjoyed by the other. Allah is enough.

المقسط جل جلاله

AL-MUQSIṬ

Allah is the one who acts and distributes in justice and fairness.

How harmonious and balanced is the creation: all the beauties in heaven and earth—mountains, seas, sunsets, flowers—and also eyes to see. If there were none to see, wouldn't the creation of all these beauties be without sense? the earth were closer to the sun all of us on its face would have burned to ashes. If it were further, we would have frozen. How right is its place. If the oxygen in the air had been more or less, it would have harmed us. Allah the Equitable One gives riches to some and poverty to others. He gives power to some, weakness to others, valor to some, fear to others. He gives what He gives to the right ones, although some may use it one way and others another way, making us doubt. We do not know what He knows, for we can see only what is in front of us, while He sees and knows the whole.

When we see laws, order and harmony in an institution, in a town, in a country, we attribute it to the existence of a just and intelligent leader. If we could see the cosmic order or the order in ourselves, who are microcosms, we would see the proof of Allah the Equitable One.

Allah treats His servants equitably. Not a single good deed goes unnoticed. Each receives a reward. Mistakes, errors, injustices are corrected. When men tyrannize each other, He takes from the tyrant and gives to the tyrannized one. Yet in doing this, He renders them both content. Only Allah can do that.

It is reported in a hadith that the Prophet (Peace and Blessings of Allah be upon him) smiled. Hz. 'Umar (May Allah be pleased with him) asked, "What is it that amuses you, O Messenger of Allah?"

The Messenger of Allah answered, "I see two men among my people who are in front of Allah Most High. One says, 'O Lord, take from this man that which is rightfully mine!' Allah Most High tells the other man, 'Give to your brother what belongs to him.' The usurper responds, 'O Lord, I have no good deeds with which to repay this man.' Allah turns to the wronged one and says, "What should I do to your brother? He has nothing left to give you.' The wronged one says, 'O Lord, let him take some of my sins.'"

With tears in his eyes, the Messenger of Allah said, "That day is the Day of Last Judgment; that day is a day when each man will wish others to carry his sins."

Then he continued to relate: "After the wronged one has wished the usurper to take over some of his sins, Allah asks him to lift his head and look at Paradise. He says, 'O Lord, I see cities of silver and palaces of gold bedecked with pearls. For which prophet, which saint, which martyr are these palaces?' Allah Most High says, 'They are for those who can pay their price.' The man who was wronged says, 'Who could possibly pay the prices of these?' Allah said, 'Perhaps you could.' The man says, 'How, O Lord? I have nothing. What could I do to gain the price of Paradise?' Allah al-Muqsit says, 'By forgiving your brother, by giving up your claim in that which he took from you.' The wronged man says, 'I forgive him, my Lord. I do not want my right.' Allah the Most Merciful, the Most Generous, says, 'Then hold your brother's hand and enter My Paradise together.'"

Then the Messenger of Allah said, "Fear Allah and fear doing harm to each other and make peace among yourselves, for Allah Most High will make peace between the believers on the Day of Last Judgment.

'Abd al-Muqsiṭ is he who has the perfect sense of measure, who sees things justly and who demands justice. Above all, he demands justice from himself. He does not demand justice from another for himself, yet he seeks justice for another from the one who has been unjust. He protects the one who should be protected. He helps the one who should be helped. He raises to the heights the ones who deserve to be elevated. The Prophet (Peace and Blessings of Allah be upon him) says, "The just will stand in pulpits of divine light in Paradise."

AL-JĀMIʿ

الجامع جل جلاله

Allah is the Gatherer of whatever He wishes, wherever He wishes.

Jama'a means gathering things that are dispersed. Allah gathers things together whether they are alike or different or even opposite. Allah has gathered together within this universe spaces, galaxies, stars, earths, seas, plants and animals, things whose nature, size, shape and color are different.

Allah has gathered in the bodies of the creatures He has created opposing entities such as fire and water, air and earth, heat and cold, dry and wet. He has gathered six million cells in a drop of blood. The body has incalculable cells, each moving, seeking, finding, rejecting, growing, dividing, dying—each a life, an entity unto itself. He has combined all those cells in the body with His knowledge and His power. He can scatter them into the far corners of the universe and gather them again. That is how our bodies, decomposed, spread in earth, water and air at death, will be gathered on the Day of Resurrection. So will the bodies of billions and billions of men. Their lives, their minds, their souls returned to them, they will be gathered in the field of Arafat on the Day of Last Judgment. Allah will gather the sinner and the pure one, the tyrant and the tyrannized, the good and the bad face to face, and judge them. Then He will gather His friends into His Paradise and His enemies into His Hell.

As Allah combines the cells of a man's body, He puts man together with his actions on the path to eternity. One's only comrades are one's deeds. In your heedlessness you do not see the flesh, the heart, the mind, the soul gathered together, and the thousands of "me"s and "I"s and "mine"s living together within you any more than you see the billions of units combined in your body. You do not see your deeds, which are with you, nor the Hell or the Paradise that is around you.

Your preoccupation with this world—eating, drinking, seeking more and more to eat, to have, to enjoy, your slavery at the hands of your flesh and your ego—have made you inattentive to everything else. Only when the bird of the soul flies from the cage of the flesh will this dream evaporate, and you will find yourself alone with your deeds. Then you will see that single companion whom you hug and press to your chest. Is it something warm and friendly or is it full of snakes and scorpions and poisonous thorns? Then you will know that what you presumed to be a good was Hell, and what you thought was suffering was Heaven.

'Abd al-Jāmi' is he in whose being visible character and morals and hidden truths of the heart are combined into one. Both his exterior and interior are beautiful. The manifestations of all the beautiful names of Allah are gathered in him. He is able to unite that which is dissimilar, different, and opposite within and outside of himself.

AL-GHANĪ

الْغَنِيُّ جَلَّ جَلَالُهُ

Allah is the Rich One who is self-sufficient.

His essence and attributes have no relationship to anything else. Someone whose existence and perfection depend on another needs to earn that existence. Only Allah needs not, neither does He need to earn. His riches are independent of others, yet all else is dependent on Him.

Allah says in Surah Muhammad, v. 38:

> . . . Allah is Self-Sufficient and you are needy.

Some men, who see themselves as superior to the rest of creation, fall into the pitiable state of arrogance and conceit. They cannot see and be thankful for the honor of being created as the supreme creation and for being given the function of being Allah's *khalīfah*—regent—in the universe.

Men's true supremacy depends on being thankful and humble, serving Allah's servants and that which Allah has placed in their charge. The arrogant, by contrast, push their conceit to the point of denying their Creator, their Lord. In their arrogance, they cannot accept to be servants of Allah. Yet they see nothing wrong with being slaves to each other!

They cannot see that even to live they need Allah's air, water, and food; as food for their souls, they need worship. In fact, in all creation, there are none whose needs are greater than man's. There is none other than Allah who is rich enough to satisfy all these needs. If Allah has sent His books and His prophets, and established religions to teach men what to do and what not to do, it is not for His need, it is for the needs of men: to enable them to exist in this world and in the Hereafter as they were meant to exist. Even the scientists, sociologists and economists of today say that the prescriptions, canons and religious laws of Allah lead men to the best of physical, moral, and economic existence. Indeed, all that Allah has created and ordered is beneficent.

To be a servant of Allah is the highest level to which a human being can aspire. When we praise our Prophet, the Beloved of Allah (Peace and Blessings of Allah be upon him), we say *'abduhu wa rasūluhu*—His servant and His messenger. The good servant of Allah knows that Allah does not need a servant, nor does He need to be served. He needs nothing. He also knows that his own duty is to serve Allah's servants and Allah's creation, including himself. Though in reality Allah has no need of servants to serve His servants—for as the Satisfier of needs, He Himself serves them—He honors whomever He chooses to appear as a means, as a tool of His service to His servants.

In reality, the good servant serves only himself in serving Allah. He obtains the greatest of gifts, coming close to Allah in knowing Him, in finding Him and in being with Him. Service and faithfulness (the quality of being a *mu'min*) become a common denominator, a common name and attribute, and thus the only means for the servant to know his Lord. When Allah addresses us in His Qur'an as "O you who believe," or "O you the believer," He calls upon us with His own attributes, with His own name, *al-Mu'min*, one of His 99 beautiful names.

Faith is a treasure from the treasury of Allah. The faithful one is the richest among men, for he knows that he needs nothing from anyone else except from Allah, the only true Rich One.

'Abd al-Ghanī is the rich one who is provided with the satisfaction of all his needs without having to ask from Allah. He does all his duties of servantship not in order to receive benefits from Allah, but only because they have been ordered by Allah.

AL-MUGHNĪ المغنى جل جلاله

Allah is the Enricher.

Allah renders whomever He wishes rich and whomever He wishes poor. Then He may render the rich, poor, and the poor, rich. Some rejoice in their riches and others suffer in their poverty. Some become conceited in their riches, some become doubtful and claim injustice in their poverty. We do not know; only He knows what is best for us. One must consider that poverty and riches, like other aspects of our lives, are but a touchstone that shows the degree of our purity. One sees in some, faithfulness, trust, and submission; in others, objection and revolt.

This life is a testing ground. Each of us comes here to show our true colors. Who we are and what we are is not measured by our bank account. There are greater riches than all the riches of this world, which may be spent, lost, taken away by others, and which will certainly be left behind when we meet our Lord. But the true riches are knowledge and faith, which do not decrease by spending, nor devaluate with time. They are our companions in the grave and in the Hereafter. The purpose of our lives is to pass this test.

Allah tests some with riches and some with poverty. What matters is submission to Allah's will. The riches of this world tempt one to revolt and to be arrogant. Poverty tempts one to doubt and to complain. It is difficult for the rich to be humble, while the poor are humble. It is difficult for the poor to accept and to be generous but easier for them to be devout.

The Prophet (Peace and Blessings of Allah be upon him) said, "My poverty is my pride." The test is not a simple test. It is not sufficient for the rich to be humble to pass the test, nor for the poor to trust in Allah and be accepting of their condition. The rich have to know thankfulness and to consider that their riches are not theirs, and to show their thankfulness by their generosity. The poor

Allāh Jāmi, Al-Ghanī, Al-Mughnī, Al-Māni', Al-Hādī

have to work hard to better their situation and accept their poverty in spite of their efforts. That is the true meaning of trust in Allah, who says, "I will not change the lot of those who do not change it themselves."

The poor who accept their state, who are content with what they have, who are not envious, are rich. The rich who are miserly, ambitious, who want more, are poor. The patient poor are bound for Paradise, as are the thankful, generous rich.

Once a pure man asked a man of knowledge what should be the attitude of the one upon whom Allah has bestowed riches and the one whom Allah has given poverty. The wise man said that the rich one should show thankfulness and the poor one should be patient. The pure believer replied that the dogs in his village behaved that way! The wise man, annoyed, asked him what he, then, thought they should do. The pure believer answered, "The poor one should be thankful and the rich one should give away all his riches."

'Abd al-Mughnī is the servant of Allah who has been rendered totally rich, both materially and spiritually, so that he becomes an instrument of satisfying the needs of the needy. He also becomes an example for other rich people to do the same. He becomes a means of distributing the riches of this world and of the Hereafter to the ones chosen by Allah.

AL-MĀNI' المانع جل جلاله

Allah is the one who averts harm from His creation.

Man is unable to do, yet we do not understand this. We wish, we will, and we try to obtain that which we wish and will. Our wishes are endless and our plans, calculations and efforts to obtain what we wish are boundless. But the obtaining of these wishes depends on many causes, effects and reasons. We do not obtain everything that we wish and work for. The causes that produce these things and bring them into being depend on the manifestation of Allah's attribute *al-Mu'tī*, the Bestower. When our wishes are not fulfilled, it is a manifestation of Allah's attribute *al-Māni'*, the Preventer. In both cases, what happens is what was bound to happen in accordance with Allah's destiny; one knows one's destiny only after it is actualized.

Allah al-Khabir is aware of our wishes. Allah al-Ghani has infinite treasuries containing what we wish. Allah al-Karim does not withhold what we wish. Allah al-Qadir is able to procure instantly what we wish. Allah is the Richest, Most Beneficent, Most Powerful, Most Just.

If we do not receive what we wish, it is not because He does not know of it, nor because He does not have it, nor because He cannot afford to give it; nor is He unable to hand it to us. He is perfect, free from all defect. Though the reason may be unknown to us, we must believe that if we do not receive what we will and wish, it is because that is best for us.

It is as if there were a perfect father who is most loving and protective to his children. He is wise, rich, generous and kind, not only to his children and his family, but to everyone. If he prevents one of his children from eating too much, or from eating an unripe fruit or from playing with a dangerous toy, can we call him lacking in compassion? Certainly he prevented the child from having or doing something with the thought of what was best for the child. Indeed, Allah's compassion is infinitely superior to that of the most compassionate of fathers.

Allah says in Surah Baqarah, v. 216:

> . . . and it may be that you dislike a thing while it is good for you, and it may be that you love a thing while it is evil for you; and Allah knows while you know not.

'Abd al-Māni' is the one who has been rendered safe by Allah from things harmful to him. He in turn protects those around him from harmful things, even though they may appear in such attractive forms as wealth, fame, beauty, joy, etc.

AḌ-ḌARR

الضَّارُّ جَلَّ جَلَالُهُ

Allah is the creator of the harmful and evil as He is the creator of the good and beneficial.

The attribute *ad-Ḍarr*, the Creator of Evil, is usually conceived together with the attribute *an-Nāfi'*, the Creator of Good. Neither name appears in the Qur'an. They belong to the attributes of Allah on the authority of the Prophet (Peace and Blessings of Allah be upon him).

Sometimes the two attributes are inseparable. What is poison to one is medicine to another. Sweet to one is bitter to another. We think that food feeds by itself and poison kills by itself. We think that the one responsible for good and evil is a man, or an angel, or the Devil, while all that happens is by the will of the Eternal Power. Although Allah has created evil as well as good, He has also taught us to opt for the good and escape the evil. He has given us the power of discrimination, given us a will and freedom to choose. In the whole creation, only man has a will. Through this will, Allah has separated mankind into two parts: the good doing good and being led towards good and the bad doing evil and being led towards evil. This—knowingly, willingly—men do themselves.

Allah Most High is *Ḥalīm*, gentle, and He is *Ṣabūr*, patient. He does not destroy those who have opted for evil. He keeps feeding them, letting them have time so that possibly they will change, which sometimes they do: the good for the worse or the evil for the better. This is all a test. The final exam is at the time one inhales one's last breath. Indeed, if a wall is cracked and leaning to the right, as time passes it will lean further and finally collapse on the right side. But, rarely, just as the wall is about to collapse to the side toward which it is leaning, an unusual thing happens. A hurricane, an earthquake, will either straighten the wall or make it collapse on the other side. Likewise the ones who revolt, who disbelieve, who become toys in the hands of their egos and the claws of the Devil, one day may feel the pang of the fear of Allah and take to the right path. Or they may appear to be like those who follow the straight path—devout, compassionate, and generous; but they start being pleased with themselves, become arrogant, think themselves better than others—and may be rejected from Allah's mercy as was the arrogant Devil.

Indeed the suffering we go through, the harm that comes to us, is only our own fault. Although Allah created evil and ordered us to shun it, forbade it to us, we run after the things that are forbidden. That is the test. We think of the Devil as an ugly creature. The Devil shows his ugliness only to the ones who detect him. When he comes to tempt even the saints, as when he appeared to Jesus Christ (May Allah bless him), he appears as a beautiful woman.

Allah has manifested His attribute of the Creator of the Harmful in the Devil and the ones who follow him; He created Hellfire for them. Although Allah created evil, the cause of its coming to you is only yourself. If bankruptcy comes upon you, it is through your dishonesty or overambitiousness or incapability. If sickness comes upon you, usually it is because of your carelessness or your negligence of your body. Although Allah has created evil, the one who wants it, works for it and gains it is the servant himself. Some serve as lessons to others, others learn from their own lessons. There is practically no one who does not slip into sinning at one time or another; he who suffers through it is the one who learns from his mistakes, for that is the best of repentance.

However, sometimes Allah Most High puts a veil of pain

and distress over the ones whom He loves and the ones who love Him to hide them from the eyes of others.

This is a blessing of Allah given through misery. Allah uses difficulty and pain as a means of educating His servants. If there were nothing negative, disturbing, or painful in the world, and if men were not afflicted by these things, how could they have gained such beneficial states as patience, perseverance, bravery, and steadfastness?

When one is afflicted with grief, fear, sickness, or poverty, know that there is none other than Allah who can dispel it. When one is blessed with happiness, health, success and riches, again only He can sustain it. Therefore, whether in health or sickness, joy or sorrow, you are bound to submit and turn only to Him, because both good and evil come from the same source. They are both true and right.

Yet this does mean that one should leave everything in the hands of Allah. One should seek the causes created by oneself or others and try to put things right in a lawful manner. To do this does not mean lack of faith in the Creator of good and evil. It is the best form of worship under the circumstances.

'Abd ad-Ḍarr is he who is a witness to the only One who does what He wills to do when He wills to do it. He is taught the mystery of the secret of the unity of all that happens. He knows that evil as well as good is from Allah and that evil as well as good is welcome.

AN-NĀFI' ٱلنَّافِعُ جَلَّ جَلَالُهُ

Allah is the creator of good.

Allah has created man as the best of His creation and He has bestowed upon him gifts which render him unique and superior to the rest of creation. The best of the gifts He has given to man are intellect, conscience, and faith. These are the means by which He taught man to discriminate and choose for himself the best of His creation. Man is also unique in that he has a will, the only one in the universe with the exception of Allah. His small will can only be checked by the greater will of Allah. This limitation means that man is not free and left on his own.

Allah has given freedom only for man to see whether he will submit to the will of Allah, be the best of creation, govern in His name and have the best of creation, or whether he will revolt, cause his own downfall, and be rejected from Allah's mercy, as was the Devil. Man's ability to choose between good and evil is not a test for Allah to see how His servant will behave. Allah created our fates before He created us; therefore, He knows.

Allah's mercy rains upon us continually, as does all the good He has created. Our will cannot bring anything to us that is due to someone else, nor can it prevent anything from coming to us that is our destiny. Neither are we able to choose, for often what we choose slips from our hands, and what we did not want comes to us. Even if we have what we choose, it would have come to us in any case.

When man looks at the universe, what he sees is Allah's will, what he sees *with* is Allah's will, what he understands of what he sees is Allah's will, what he seems to have chosen is Allah's will. His small will consists of being able to open his eyes to receive all the good that Allah has willed for him, or to close his eyes and receive nothing. It is as if the treasures of Allah are pouring continuously like a blessed rain. We have to be present to receive it. If we are not there, it will go to waste. To be present, we have to open our eyes, our minds, our hearts, and our hands. We have to be aware, awake, conscious. That is how we see and receive the good that Allah has created.

'Abd an-Nāfi' is he who sees and receives the good Allah has created and is charged with distributing the beneficences of Allah—the greatest of which are knowledge and faith—to the ones worthy to receive. He is like Khidr, and follows his path and example.

AN-NŪR

النُّورُ جَلَّ جَلَالُهُ

Allah is the the Light that is shed upon the whole creation, making it apparent.

Just as this Light is responsible for making the perceptible seen, it also makes the conceivable known. The light that shows the perceptible is the light of faith and wisdom, and the eye that sees it is the *baṣīrah*, the eye of the heart. That Light is the light of existence; nonexistence is darkness. That Light makes itself visible as well as making all else visible. That Light is the light that brought existence out of the darkness of nonexistence. There is not one atom among all the things that exist in the heavens and on earth and in that which is between them that does not point to the existence of its Creator, " . . . the Light of the heavens and the earth." (Surah Nur, v. 35).

The sun sheds light upon the sky and the earth, enabling us to see things around us—large and small, of different shapes and colors—enabling us to identify that from which we may profit and that which may harm us. In that light we find our way and see the pits and swamps. In the same way, Allah has bestowed upon us the light of faith, which shows us the straight path of salvation and the pits and swamps of infidelity, sin and revolt. That sun of faith in the heart of the believer renders him beautiful of face and beautiful in character. The light of faith eliminates the darknesses of infidelity and sin within and without, bringing one to the light of truth and salvation and serenity.

The Devil, and one's own devil, the ego, are thieves who like to operate in darkness and enter dark houses. They will not enter that divine house, the heart illuminated by the light of faith. The gate to the heart is the mind; the light of that gate is knowledge; that light blocks out the evil of ignorance, imagination, hypocrisy and arrogance. The soul needs light and detests darkness. As the light of the soul is consciousness, its darkness is heedlessness.

You who spend so much effort and wealth to illuminate your material life with chandeliers, sparkling jewels and bright ostentation, why do you turn off the light of your heart? Don't you see that you may cause it to become used to darkness, and go blind like the bat? If the eye of your head goes blind, someone may lead you by the hand on the road; but the one whose heart is blind cannot be led and will be lost for eternity.

'Abd an-Nūr is the servant of Allah who has received the blessing of a response to the prayer of the Prophet Muhammad (Peace and Blessings of Allah be upon him), "O My Lord, render me light," and who has come to know the secret of the verse of the Qur'an, "Allah is the Light of heavens and earth." He knows that all existence, knowledge, thought and feeling come from that light, and that all existence and knowledge in the universe are nothing but that light.

AL-HĀDĪ الهادي جل جلاله

Allah is the one who creates guidance, leading His servants to good, beneficence and the satisfaction of their needs.

First of all He guides His best servants to knowledge of His essence. Then He guides His other good servants to see the things in His creation that manifest His attributes. He guides every creature to that which is needed for its existence.

Allah says in Surah Ta Ha, v. 50:

Our Lord is He Who gives to each thing its nature
then guides it (to knowledge to satisfy its needs).

The result of this guidance is faith. The opposite of guidance is to be led astray, the result of which is infidelity.

Man is made like a pair of scales. He has the potential to go one way or the other. Therefore, for him to go either to the side of faith or to the side of infidelity there must be some weight placed on one side of the scale or the other. Allah is the only one who has created guidance and misguidance. He is the creator of the causes of faith, which delights the heart, and of faithlessness, which delights the ego. He guides whomever He wishes and leads astray whomever He wishes.

Whomever Allah has guided well, none can lead astray. Whomever Allah has misguided, none can lead to the straight path. But Allah does not forcibly and without reason lead His servant astray. He leads man astray only when he misuses his will and turns his potential towards infidelity. Yet in man, faith is essential, fundamental. Faithlessness is nonessential and accidental.

Faith is essential in man. Allah gathered the souls prior to creation in the realm of the spirits and asked, "Am I not your Lord?" and we all answered, "Indeed!" So our souls have a covenant with Allah. We may not remember the promise of our souls, but that does not invalidate the pact. It is this covenant with Allah before our creation that is the reason for Allah's guidance and bounty for each soul. He has granted a perfect body to live in, sustenance for the maintenance of that body, a mind to perceive things which will remind one of His existence and of our covenant with Him. He has given the Books, the Messengers, prophets and saints and men of knowledge, to remind, to teach, to confirm the covenant. All this is a part of Allah's guidance. As man wishes it, wills it and abides with it, Allah's guidance will ever increase.

The one who is well guided knows the truth, respects the truth, accepts the truth. He will prefer death to the application of untruth, which is injustice and tyranny. Even if he had the interest, strength, and support to go against the truth, he would not do it. He tells only the truth, listens to the truth, lives by the truth and dies for the truth. That is the well-guided one.

'Abd al-Hādī is the servant of Allah who has received the response to his prayer (Fatiha, v.5), "Guide us on the right path." He knows the secret of the beautiful name *al-Hādī*, and thus becomes an instrument for man's salvation. He has been charged with enforcing truth: that which Allah ordains, and that which Allah forbids.

AL-BADĪ' البديع جل جلاله

Allah is the Originator of the creation, having created it without model or material.

He does not need previous knowledge to think, to first investigate, to figure things out. He invents the first of everything in the creation. There was nothing before Him, so He is unlike anything, and everything after Him is made by Him—unique, matchless, unequalled by anything else, and in no way similar to Him. Everything He creates is a wonder, a marvel, since He originated it from nothing. Like the original creations, all the continuous created things are different from each other. Although they resemble each other, they are also different from each other. There are no two men exactly alike.

A man marveled to the caliph, Hz. 'Umar (May Allah be pleased with him), about the chess game. "Look at this board, not bigger than a foot square," he said. "A man can play thousands of games on it, none like any other!"

Hz. 'Umar (May Allah be pleased with him) said, "Why don't you look at a man's face, which is smaller than the chessboard? Although the eyes, the nose, the mouth are always in the same place, if you look at millions of men, you will not find two alike. And when you add the variety of expressions, there is no end to the differences, as there is no end to the power and wisdom and the originality of Allah Most High."

Attention and curiosity are two of the greatest gifts to man. All knowedge, science, industry, are inventions of these qualities. Man cannot invent or originate; all he can do is discover things that Allah has previously created. As man observes phenomena with his attention and investigates with his curiosity, seeing the model of the bird and the fish, using the minerals and materials available to him, he discovers airplanes and submarines. Some stop there, profiting from the material gains and fame, and become arrogant, thinking that *they* have invented and *they* have created. Blessed are those scientists and inventors who use their success as an introduction to the greater success of receiving the love of Allah in their hearts; they see the Hand of Power of Allah the Originator and Allah the All-Powerful, who has used them as tools to bring about their discoveries.

How well have the wise ones said, "The ones who work with divine wisdom are light, the ones who practice knowledge are guides, the ones who give good advice are lamps, the ones who think and know are alive, the ones who are ignorant are dead."

'Abd al-Badi' is the witness that Allah Most High is the creator of everything in its essence, attributes, and actions. He is given the ability to know, to discover, and to build things that others cannot.

AL-BĀQĪ

الْبَاقِي جَلَّ جَلَالُهُ

Allah is the Everlasting One whose existence in the future is forever.

He is after the after; He is also before the before. He has neither beginning nor end. Time only exists for the changing creation. It started with His word of creation and will end on Doomsday. There was no time before the creation, but Allah existed. The creation will end, and time with it. But Allah the Everlasting One will still exist.

This world is but a guest house where the visitor stays for awhile, then leaves. For millenia, how many visitors have come and gone. Who were they? Where are they? Where did they go? Nations and civilizations have come and gone. Man and everything else in the universe is like this; but for man, this world is also a field where he labors to grow wheat or thorns, and whose harvest he will find in the Hereafter. This life is like a parade ground; everyone passes as his turn comes, all in different groups, under different banners, with different uniforms, marching to different music. No one is left in this world, nor is this world left with anyone. All is material, temporal—including the world itself, the whole universe—except Allah the Everlasting One.

Yet there is a way to gain an eternal life during this short visit here. It is achieved by not tying one's heart to this world. It is by not working only for profit in this world, by not working for one's own immediate benefit. If one works for Allah's sake, for Allah's pleasure, for the benefit of Allah's creation now and in the future, when all is ended and this body has returned to dust one's work will carry one to eternity.

If you are a doctor or an architect, when you go to that realm where there is no one who is sick and nothing to build, both your being and your knowledge will disappear. But if you discovered penicillin, which will keep curing the sick long after you are gone, or if you built a bridge which people will cross for a long time, and if your intention in doing these things was to serve rather than to gain, you will earn eternity in the Hereafter for what you have done in this temporal life.

'Abd al-Bāqī is the good servant of Allah who is given the knowledge of eternity, whom Allah has rendered eternal within His eternity in the state of *baqā' billāh*. In that state, his worship is his servantship, where the servant and the Lord have become one, and there is nothing left of the servant himself.

AL-WĀRITH الوارث جل جلاله

Allah is the ultimate Inheritor, to whom everything is left after its temporal possessors are gone.

It is He who exists after all existence disappears; it is He to whom all existence returns. It is He who will ask:

> To whom belongs the kingdom this day?

And it is He who will answer:

> To Allah, the One, the Ever-Dominating One.
> (Surah Mu'minun, v.16)

The heedless one is unaware that what he possesses, including himself, is only lent to him. The one who is not thankful for the infinite bounties of Allah the Most Generous One is arrogant, thinking that what he has is his. He uses it for his own pleasure. When he disappears, he and all else return to Allah the Everlasting One, who is before the before and after the after, who is the only Owner, the Inheritor of all. Then he will be asked:

> To whom belongs the kingdom this day?

And he will know the truth, only too late.

But the ones whose eyes of the heart see and whose ears of the heart hear, remember and hear continuously:

To Allah, the One, the Ever-Dominating One.

They know that they are but temporal keepers of what is in their hands. They are as if honored tellers of Allah's bank, who do not follow the desires of their flesh nor the commands of their egos, but do what Allah wills for His sake and for His pleasure. In that, they become one with Allah and become eternal and everlasting.

'Abd al-Wārith is the servant who attains the secret of the name the Inheritor, who is in the state of *baqā' billāh*, "everlastingness with Allah," and who receives his share of divine wisdom and of the station of the prophets. *'Abd al-Warith* is the inheritor of the prophets in knowledge, wisdom and guidance.

AR-RASHĪD

الرشيد جل جلاله

Allah is the Righteous Teacher who ordains righteousness for all creatures.

In His wisdom He leads all matters to their finality in a perfect way and order. He is the ultimate teacher who leads one to the straight path and salvation. He is a perfect teacher who never fails in His wisdom or in His actions. Everything done by Him has a clear and beneficial purpose. His teaching is so effective that it becomes the nature of everything in the universe that follows His will.

To man He has taught bliss, prosperity, and salvation in His Qur'an. He does not enforce what He teaches, but leaves it to man's will to act upon what he is taught. He shows the way to peace, bliss and prosperity as a reward for acting upon what He teaches. Although Allah the All-Powerful is able to enforce His commands, He chooses to let man gain his rewards by his own decision in acting upon what he is taught.

Allah Al-Wārith, Aṣ-Ṣabūr, Ar-Rashīd

Man as the student first has to be aware and conscious of what is being taught. Then he has to use the intelligence that has been given to him by his teacher to discipline and educate himself, his ego. Then he has to learn Allah's divine laws, and in accordance with them, drive the machine of his material being.

Islam is the religion in which learning is obligatory for all men and women. As they learn from Allah the ultimate Righteous Teacher, they see the perfect order within and outside themselves. The Greatest Teacher makes His students see His Will, His Power, His Generosity, His Love, His Compassion. He makes the student love Him, live to do what He says, love to work for His pleasure and to become righteous.

'Abd ar-Rashīd is the righteous one who has arrived at the right path that leads to Allah's will and His Messenger's orders. This is the station of the *murshid*, the great teacher who has come to know, to find, and to become close to Allah. As he is on the straight path, he also has the license to lead others on the straight path.

AS-ṢABŪR الصبور جل جلاله

Allah is the Most Patient One.

In everything He is in perfect measure and in perfect time. He is patient, and He loves and . . .

is with the patient ones.

(Surah Anfal, v.46)

In His creation as in His actions, in His dealings with His creation, nothing is either bigger or smaller, better or worse, earlier or later than it is determined for it to be. He does not delay things beyond their appointed times or fail to finish them as a lazy one might do, nor does He hasten and imperfectly finish things as an impatient one might do. Rather he does everything in its proper time and in just the manner that it ought to be done.

Allah does not hasten the punishment of the sinful. He sends them their sustenance, protects them from harm, and lets them live in health and prosperity, for He has set a determined time for everything. Everything has to run its course. His patience with sinners is in order to give them time to be heedful, to realize their wrong and come to repent. Allah is Merciful; His Mercy is in giving time for repentance and accepting repentance.

Patience is in Allah's divine disposition; therefore, patient men reflect this honored disposition. A patient man is he who refuses things that his flesh and ego desire but that are unacceptable to reason and to the religion; he applies himself to things that are acceptable in the religion and to reason, yet hateful for his ego, as he knows how to put a bridle on the wild horse of his flesh and his ego.

Patience is a very high state for the believer, because the affairs both of this world and of the Hereafter are resolved by it. No success, no perfection, can be achieved easily and without pain. That pain is the pain of the flesh, which is hasty in things that it wants, which is lazy in working for what it wants, which does not know measure and always wants more than it needs.

The Prophet (Peace and Blessings of Allah be upon him) says that, "Paradise is surrounded by things that the flesh does not want." Allah promises infinite rewards for those who can be patient with the turbulence of the desires of their flesh and of their egos. There are even greater rewards for patience in supporting misfortunes, poverty, accidents, and sickness, which are unavoidable and come from Allah. Indeed calamities come from Allah, but rewards for being patient and accepting them accompany them. If people show patience, they receive rewards that far surpass the pain. If they are impatient, the misfortune doubles—first the initial calamity and then the greater misfortune of having lost the reward.

The meaning of Islam is submission: to forego one's appetites, desires and will in favor of the will of Allah. To be able to submit, one has to be patient. In Islam, patience is a sign of faith; abasement and humiliation are sins. Do not confuse humiliation caused by fear and laziness with patience and endurance. To give up one's property, one's honor, one's dignity to a tyrant may lead one to give up one's religion and faith for fear, or to sell one's soul for this world. The believer who fears Allah fears no one, and is one whom others fear. For him to abase himself before anyone except Allah is not lawful.

'Abd aṣ-Ṣabūr is the blessed servant who has perfect equilibrium and moderation in himself and in all that he does, who neither delays nor hastens, but acts in a determined time. He is patient in his continuous battle with his ego and in the opposition of his desires and appetites. He perseveres in keeping Allah's ordinances and in his worship.

O Lord, for the sake of Your beautiful names,
and for the sake of the ones
in whom Your names are manifest,
lead us on their path. Let us see
your attributes everywhere without,
and cleanse the mirror of our hearts
that perchance we may see Your Beauty reflected within.

Amīn bi ḥurmati sayyid al-mursalīn.

The Divine Names of the Prophet

(Peace and Blessings of Allah be upon him)

BISMILLĀH AR-RAḤMĀN AR-RAḤĪM

O Allah, for as long as day turns to night and night recedes into day, for as long as the ages succeed one another, as day and night unceasingly follow upon each other and as the glowing stars remain suspended in the firmament, we beg that You bestow Your grace and favors upon our Master Muhammad and that You transmit unto his blessed soul and unto the souls of the people of his house our greetings and our respect, and that You bestow upon him Your peace and blessings in great abundance.

So may Allah bestow His peace and blessings upon our Master Muhammad and upon all the prophets and messengers; upon the saints and the righteous servants; upon the angels and upon those who reside by the Throne of Grace; and upon the obedient and vigilant servants among the people of the earth and those of the skies. And may Allah Most High be pleased with His Prophet and with all His companions and people. Amin.

He is the one who is "sent as a mercy upon the universe" (Surah Anbiya', 107). The light of his soul was the first creation from the light of Allah, and all else is created from his light. He said, "O Jabir, the first creation that Allah created is the soul of your prophet." When he was asked when he became a prophet, he answered, "I was a prophet when Adam was between water and clay." He said, "Whoever sees me sees the truth."

Allah says:

> And whoever obeys Allah and His Messenger, He will cause him to enter gardens wherein rivers flow.
>
> (Surah Fath, 17)

And he has said, "As long as you do not love me more than anything else you have, your faith is not complete." For

Allah says:

> Certainly a Messenger has come to you from amongst yourselves; grievous to him is your falling into distress; most solicitous for you; to the believers he is merciful.
>
> (Surah Bara'at, 128)

He upon whom "Allah has bestowed the noblest of characters and most excellent of actions," is sent to teach us to be noble in behavior, morals, and character. "Whoever prays to Allah to bestow upon His Messenger His peace and blessings, receives Allah's blessings tenfold, and may hope for the intercession of His Prophet on the Day of Last Judgment, and to enter Paradise."

We are presenting 201 beautiful names of our beloved Prophet (Peace and Blessings of Allah be upon him) as mentioned in the *Dalā'il al-khayrāt* of Shaykh 'Imran al-Zannati, may his soul be sanctified. Allah praises His Prophet with most of these names in the Holy Qur'an, and announces his coming by certain names in the other Holy Books: the *Torah*, the *Zabur (Psalms of David)*, and the *Gospel.* They also appear in the Hadith, or traditions of the Prophet (Peace and Blessings of Allah be upon him).

Shaykh Ibn al-Faris reports from Hz. Ibn al-'Arabi that he had counted 2,020 beautiful attributes of our Prophet (Peace and Blessings of Allah be upon him). Imam al-Kastalani, the author of the interpretation of *Bukhari al-Sharif,* the collections of Hadith, has counted 1,000 beautiful names.

May the ones who read the beautiful names of the Beloved of Allah (Peace and Blessings of Allah be upon him) contemplate the meaning, properties and effects of these names and feel the love, the respect, and the consideration with which we hope their hearts will be inspired. We must realize that to love is not within our will, but within the greater will of Allah. He is the One Who inspires the heart with love. By ourselves we cannot love Allah and His Prophet; by ourselves a man cannot even love a woman, or a woman, a man. In Islam it is unlawful for a man to insist that his wife love him or for a wife to insist upon the affection of her husband, for that is considered equal to forcing one to lie. As one cannot be forced to love, nor can one force onself to love someone, how then should we understand the Hadith, "If you do not love me more than anything else you have, your faith is not complete"? First is the wish, which can only be obtained through knowing him, through knowing his beautiful names, through finding a trace of these attributes in your own selves, through praying for him and for his blessings, through following his path and his example. Then, if Allah wills, you will be blessed with his love, and in return, you will love him and find Paradise in this world and in the Hereafter.

'Ali ibn Abu Talib (May Allah be pleased with him) said in describing the Prophet (Peace and Blessings of Allah be upon him):

> He was neither tall and lanky nor short and stocky, but of medium height. His hair was neither crisply curled nor straight but moderately wavy. He was not overweight, and his face was not plump. He had a round face. His complexion was white tinged with reddishness. He had big black eyes with long lashes. His bones were heavy and his shoulders broad. He had soft skin, with fine hair covering the line from midchest to navel. The palms of his hands and the soles of his feet were firmly padded. He walked with a firm gait, as if striding downhill. On his back between his shoulders lay the Seal of Prophethood, for he was the last of the prophets.
>
> He was the most generous of men in feeling, the most truthful in speech, the gentlest in disposition, and the noblest in lineage. At first encounter people were awestruck by him, but on closer acquaintance they would come to love him. One who sought to describe him could only say, "Neither before him nor after him did I ever see the like of him."

O Allah, bless and salute the Prophet of Mercy, the intercessor of the community, Muhammad, and all his family and all the prophets and messengers.

His being was of light; he had no shadow. His beautiful face shone like the sun and radiated light around him. At night people saw by this light. It is written in the Holy Qur'an that in the darkness of the Day of Last Judgment the light of faith of the believers is going to illuminate the space around them, and the hypocrites, envious, will come close to them to profit from this light.

Allah, addressing His Beloved, whose name is written with His upon the firmament as *Lā ilāha illāllāh, Muḥammadun rasūlullāh*—"There is no god worthy of worship except Allah, and Muhammad is His Messenger"—says,"If it were not for you, I would not have created the creation." Therefore the greatest gift bestowed by Allah upon the universe is His Beloved. He says in the Holy Qur'an:

> And if you count Allah's favors, you will not be able to number them.
>
> (Surah Ibrahim, 34)

Thus if we try to count the beautiful attributes of our beloved Prophet (Peace and Blessings of Allah be upon him), the best of Allah's favors, we will be unable to number them.

1. **Muḥammad** The most praised one

He is praised upon earth and in the heavens, from the beginning to the end, by men and jinn and angels, rocks and trees and animals, by prophets before him since Adam, by saints until Doomsday. As all of this cannot give him due praise, we beg Allah to praise him. He is the only One who truly knows the value and the mystery of His Muhammad (Peace and Blessings of Allah be upon him), and He is the only One who can truly praise him.

2. **Aḥmad** The most praiseworthy of those who praise Allah

This is the celestial name of the Prophet (Peace and Blessings of Allah be upon him). Allah, the Ever-Existing, the All-Powerful, 360,000 years before He created the creation, created from His divine light a sacred light. That light upon light praised Allah before and during the creation of heaven and the heavenly and earth and the earthly. The inhabitants of the heavens named that light *Aḥmad*. As his praise of Allah is greater than the praise of all that is created, he is called *aḥmad al-ḥāmidin*—the greatest of givers of praise.

Aḥmad is the name by which he is mentioned in the Gospel.

> And when Jesus son of Mary said, "O Children of Israel, surely I am the Messenger of Allah to you, verifying that which is before me of the Torah and giving good news of a Messenger who will come after me, his name being Ahmad."
>
> (Surah Saff, 6)

In the Bible, Jesus (May Allah bless him) says:

> I have yet many things to say unto you, but ye cannot bear them now. Howbeit when he, the Spirit of Truth, is come, he will guide you unto all truth, for he shall not speak of himself, but whatsoever he shall hear, that shall he speak; and he

will show you things to come. He shall glorify me.

(John 14:17)

That Spirit of Truth who speaks but Allah's words is Ahmad.

3. **Ḥamīd** The only one who is given the ability to praise and give thanks to Allah

He is the one who will praise Allah on the Day of Last Judgment, just as he praised Allah as the first created light. On that Day he will put his blessed face on the ground in prostration, praise the Lord, and beg mercy for us. *Ḥamīd* (Peace and Blessings of Allah be upon him) says, On that day my Lord will enable me to praise Him as I never did before, and I will praise Him more than I did ever before. Then He will tell me, "Lift your head, My Beloved. I promised that

I will give to thee so that thou wilt be well pleased

(Duha, 5)

and I accept your intercession for your people until you are satisfied. Your praises are accepted, your intercession is accepted."

4. **Maḥmūd** The praised one

He is praised by all who are raised on the Day of Last Judgment, for he will be the only one who will intercede for the believers and whose intercession will be valid. He is the one who has been raised to the station of great glory—*al-maqām al-maḥmūd*. Allah asked His Beloved

During a part of the night keep awake and pray, beyond what is encumbent on thee. Maybe thy Lord will raise thee to *maqaman mahmudan* (a station of glory).

(Bani Isra'il, 79)

Maḥmūd is the name with which he is mentioned in the Psalms of David.

5. **Aḥīd** The only one who will protect his people from Hellfire

On the day when sinners will be thrown into Hellfire, Allah will address *Aḥīd* (Peace and Blessings of Allah be upon him), and say, "O My Beloved, these are the ones who have denied Us and revolted against Us, because they have denied you, disobeyed you, and not followed you. You can use the Hellfire as you wish upon them. And these are the ones who said they believed in and obeyed you, but succumbed to the temptation of the accursed Devil and the desires of their flesh, and sinned. You can use My Hellfire upon them, or free them." He is the key that locks the seven doors of Hell, he is the key that opens the eight doors of Paradise, he is the mercy of Allah upon the universe.

When Allah willed to take His Beloved to Himself, He sent the angel Gabriel (May Allah bless him) who said, "Allah Most High asks you—when He takes your soul, where in His Paradise do you wish your body to rest?"

At this the heavens, in great pride and joy, declared, "The suns are within us, the moons and the stars are within us, the Throne and Canopy and the Kaaba in the seventh heaven and Paradise are within us, and Muhammad will be within us!"

The Mercy Upon the Universe asked, "O my brother Gabriel, where will my people be buried?"

Gabriel answered, "Surely under this earth, O Messenger of Allah."

The Beloved of Allah said, "In that case, I ask to be buried here with them, so that I will be with them when we are raised."

Then this world with joy declared, "O heavens, the suns, the moons, the stars, the Throne, the Kaaba of the seventh heaven, and Paradise may be in you, but the Beloved of Allah is within me!"

6. **Waḥid** The unique one

He is unique among men. He has come among us as a man like us, most beautiful in form and character, the gentlest, the highest in knowledge and wisdom. But his uniqueness is his station bestowed upon him by the Creator. As Allah embued Adam with the knowledge of all the Names, Allah gave the Last of the Prophets the knowledge of all the Names, all the Attributes, and all Essence. These he had had since the creation of his light as the first creation. He saw them with his own eyes upon his ascension. He saw even his Lord, who is free of all dimensions.

7. **Māḥī** The annihilator of the darkness of faithless and heedlessness

He is the one who came to a world immersed in darkness, filled with tyranny, idolatry, denial, depravity, and disorder. He was sent as the mercy of the Creator upon the whole universe, and with the light of his message the tyranny turned into peace, the darkness into light, denial into faith, depravity into purity, and disorder into harmony. With his teaching, the darkness and depravity were annihilated and the world was enlightened with the light of faith, knowledge, and wisdom. The sins and revolts of the believers disappeared with the love, respect, and obedience which he inspired for Allah and for himself, and the love and care which he inspired in man for man.

8. **Ḥāshir** The gatherer, the unifier, under whom all will reassemble here and on the Day of Last Judgment

He is the one who fortold that all men—who are created Muslims, submissive to Allah, and then with their worldly environment assume false identities—will soon realize and gather under one Allah and the final message brought by him. All believers will also gather around him under the shade of his banner of grace, hoping for his intercession on the Day of Last Judgment.

9. **'Āqib** The successor of all the prophets; the final prophet

Allah says:

Muhammad . . . is the Messenger of Allah and the

Seal of the prophets . . . .

(Ahzab, 40)

No other Messenger will come after him until Doomsday, as his message will stay intact and unchanged until the end of time. He is called *'Āqib* because the totality of good character, morals, and deeds is complete within him. Neither the degree of perfection in mankind nor their closeness to their Creator can surpass his.

This name will be remembered and mentioned by the inhabitants of Hell, as the sinners among his followers will be thrown into Hell, and after their punishment will be made known to him. At this he will intercede and beg for mercy for them and save them. Then that place in Hell where the Muslims met their temporary punishment will lose its fire and be closed.

10. **Ṭā Hā** The pure purifier and the guide to true faith

Ṭā Hā is the name of a chapter of the Holy Qur'an and one of the Names of Allah. Allah honors His Beloved Prophet by some of His own names and attributes.

The ones who know say that the letters "T" and "A" of *Ṭā* stand for *Ṭāhir*, the pure and purified. The letter "H" and "A" of *Hā* stand for *Hādī*, the guide. He is the pure one who has helped purify men from faithlessness, sin, and error, and who has led them from heedlessness and ignorance into the straight path to the truth.

"T" also stands for *ṭūbā* of *ṭūbā li-man hudiya bihi*— "blessings upon those who have been guided by him"—while "H" stands for *Hādī*, the guide. Good tidings to those who have found the true path to Allah's pleasure and Paradise through believing in, loving, and obeying the Messenger of Allah.

In the system that assigns numerical values to Arabic letters, "T" equals 9 and "H" equals 5, totalling 14, the number of the day of the lunar cycle when the moon is full. This indicates that his light is like the full moon, eliminating the darkness of unconsciousness, faithlessness, and ignorance.

11. **Yā Sīn** The Perfect Man, who is master of all men

Yā Sīn is the name of a chapter in the Qur'an that is considered to be the heart of the Holy Book. It is also one of the Names of Allah. It is said that the letters "Y" and "S" stand for *yā insān*, "O Man"—the best of all men, past, present, and future. It also means the master of all men. Allah has given him a name from among His own Names because the truth of Muhammad can be truly known to Him alone.

12. **Ṭāhir** Pure and clean

He is not only cleansed from moral and spiritual stains but also from material dirt. He is clean in this world and in the other—in his faith, in his worship, in everything he did, in everything he said. His breath, his spittle, his blood were pure. At the battle of Uhud, when his blessed cheek was wounded, Malik ibn Sinan (May Allah be pleased with him), one of the Companions, pressed his mouth to the wound and swallowed the blood. The Prophet (Peace and Blessings of Allah be upon him) did not stop him from doing this, but said, "O Malik that blood you swallowed will bring you health in this world, and will protect you against Hellfire in the Hereafter."

13. **Muṭahhar** The one who is rendered pure by Allah

As *Muṭahhar*, he purifies those who follow him from disbelief, sin, the dirt of the world and the desires of the flesh. He polishes them with the light of Allah's unity and perfumes them with the love of their Lord and their Prophet. On the Day of Last Judgment he will cleanse us of all the afflictions of this world and the Hereafter, and save us from purification by Hellfire.

14. **Ṭayyib** The pleasant and beautifully fragrant one

His blessed body smelled more beautiful than the pink roses of May. When he caressed the head of a child or held someone's hand, his fragrance remained for a long time. People knew where he had passed because his fragrance lingered in the air. His wives put his perspiration upon themselves as the best of perfumes.

15. **Sayyid** The Prince of the Universe, the highest of the prophets

Many who know have interpreted this name in different ways.

"*Sayyid* is he who is gracious in the opinion of Allah." ('Abdullah ibn Abbas,(May Allah be pleased with him))

"*Sayyid* is he whose worship is complete, who is pious and chaste, who does not take revenge against injustice and tyranny but forgives, who deals gently even with his enemies." (Qatadah,(May Allah be pleased with him))

"*Sayyid* is he whose state is equal, whether he is pleased or angry." ('Ikrimah, (May Allah be pleased with him))

The Prophet himself has said, "I am the *sayyid*, master, of all men on the Day of Last Judgment," as Allah calls Himself

. . . *Māliki yawm al-dīn*

(Fatihah, 3)

"I am the Owner, the Judge on the Day of Last Judgment."

Can you think of the awe and dread of that day whose judge is Allah, and the grandeur and majesty of the one who is master of all men on that day? On that day, when all men are raised, when a thousand feet will stand on one foot, when men are trembling with fear, immersed in their own sweat, brains boiling in their skulls, all hoping for each others' aid—mothers, fathers, priests, popes, saints, even all the prophets thinking of their own salvation, and unable to help. The Beloved of Allah, the Master of the Day of Last Judgment, will be the only one to turn to for help.

16. **Rasūl** The Messenger of Allah

Allah says:

> Certainly you have in the Messenger of Allah an excellent example.
>
> (Ahzab, 26)

17. **Nabī** The Prophet who speaks Allah's words

Allah describes His Prophet Muhammad, saying,

> O Prophet, surely We have sent thee as a witness and a bearer of good news and a warner.
>
> And as an inviter to Allah by His permission, and as a light-giving sun.
>
> (Ahzab, 45-6)

18. **Rasūl ar-raḥmah** The Messenger of the Most Compassionate

Allah the Merciful, the Forgiver, addresses us through His Messenger:

> Say: O My servants who have transgressed against their souls, despair not of the mercy of Allah, for Allah forgives all sins. For He is the Oft-Forgiving, Most Merciful.
>
> (Zumar, 53)

And Allah also says of His Prophet:

> And We sent thee not but as a mercy upon the universe.
>
> (Anibya', 107)

Allah does not punish the sins of the believers, but delays the punishment also of the nonbeliever until his death, for the sake of this Messenger whom He has sent as His mercy upon the whole of creation.

19. **Qayyim** The right and good one who loves and is generous to all men

He also teaches his followers brotherhood and love for each other, gives to them, and teaches them to give to each other what is needed in this world and in the Hereafter.

20. **Jāmi'** The one in whom all knowledge is gathered

Allah has taught Hadrat Adam (May Allah be pleased with him) all the words, and the names of all that exists from the beginning to the end, and He has taught Hadrat Ibrahim (May Allah bless him) all the attributes. In

His last prophet He gathered all the knowledge of all the names, all the attributes, and the Essence. Muhammad (Peace and Blessings of Allah be upon him) not only knew them, but saw them and lived them during his ascension in the Night Journey, when he visited all the heavens, met the souls of all the prophets, saw the hundred levels of eight paradises and seven hells, and spoke 90,000 words with his Lord.

21. **Muqtafī** The last one, who follows and contains all the prophets

The Last of the Prophets has said:

> "The resemblance between me and the other prophets is like a beautiful house which is complete except for a last brick. All who see this marvel at its beauty, but are also shocked by the missing brick. With me, that building of prophethood is completed."

He is the mercy upon the universe. Allah has wished to seal His messages with a Messenger who is His Mercy. Allah has honored the followers of His last prophet by making them the last community, so that their sins and errors are hidden from the previous Messengers. Allah has made their punishment light, His rewards for them greater, and their time of waiting until the Day of Last Judgment shorter.

22. **Muqaffī** The one behind whom are all the other prophets, who follow him and are confirmed in him

The Blessed Prophet has said:

> Allah Most High has honored me to be at the head of all. No prophet has reached to my level of closeness with Allah. They are all behind me, and they all follow me in all their natural and spiritual actions and merits in this world and in the Hereafter.

23. **Rasūl al-malāḥim** Messenger to the warriors of truth

Those who are honored to follow the most merciful,

compassionate, and gentlest of prophets are the fiercest warriors against the tyranny of the nonbelievers over the believers. This *jihād* is ordered by Allah and helped by Allah. One of the miracles of Islam is the repeated victory of a handfull of Muslim warriors during the short period of 25 years over the then greatest powers of the world, the Sassanids of Persia and the Byzantines.

Within the first 40 years of the Islamic era, the whole of the Arabian Peninsula, Egypt and North Africa, Persia and Asia Minor, and the Caucasus were in Muslim hands.

That which rendered the believers victorious was Allah's help and their faith in Him. But the Prophet (Peace and Blessings of Allah be upon him) has said that the greater battle is the war with one's own ego and one's own devil, and the greatest victory is won over one's own faithlessness.

24. **Rasūl ar-rāḥah** The Messenger of appeasement and quietude

25. **Kāmil** The perfect one

26. **Iklīl** The crown of the believers

27. **Muddaththir** The one who shows patience towards those who tyrannize him

Because he was patient toward those who were hostile, he has been addressed in the Qur'an as:

> O thou wrapped up [in a mantle] . . . for thy Lord's cause be patient and constant.
>
> (Muddaththir 1,7)

28. **Muzammil** The one who wraps himself up in his cloak as he did in the awe of the first revelation

29. **'Abdullāh** Allah's ultimate servant

With this name he has received the highest honor, as to be the true servant of Allah is the highest level to which any human being may aspire.

30. **Ḥabībullāh** The Beloved of Allah

This name is proper only to him.

31. **Ṣafiyullāh** The chosen of Allah out of the whole creation

He was purified, sustained, brought up, and educated by Allah Himself. From him all that is lacking was taken away, and to him all perfection was given.

32. **Najī'ullāh** The deliverer who leads to salvation

33. **Kalīmullāh** The one who converses with Allah

He spoke 90,000 words with Allah in his ascension during the Night Journey.

34. **Khātim al-anbiyā'** The Seal of the Prophets, with whom all prophethood is fulfilled

Allah declares:

> Muhammad . . . is the apostle of Allah and the seal of the prophets.
>
> (Ahzab, 40)

35. **Khātim ar-rusul** The Seal of the Messengers

36. **Muḥyī** The vivifier of dead hearts with the light of faith

37. **Munjī** The one who delivers from sin

38. **Mudhakkir** The one who reminds us of the Creator and of the Day of Last Judgment

39. **Nāṣir** The helper of men, the ally of the righteous

40. **Manṣūr** The one made triumphant in this world and in the Hereafter

He is the one fortified by the assistance of Gabriel and other angels, and by Allah Himself.

41. **Nabī ar-raḥmah** The prophet who was sent as Allah's mercy upon the universe

42. **Nabī at-tawbah** The prophet of repentance, striving for man's welfare

43. **Ḥarīṣ 'alaykum** The one filled with solicitude for you

Mentioned in the Qur'an as the one zealous for your salvation. Allah says:

> . . . It grieves him that ye should perish; ardently anxious is he over you; to the believers is he most kind and merciful.
>
> (Tawbah, 128)

44. **Ma'lūm** The well-known

45. **Shahīr** The celebrated one

46. **Shāhid** The witness

47. **Shahīd** The martyr

48. **Mashshūd** The witnessed

49. **Bashīr** The sender of good news to the believers

50. **Mubashshir** The bringer of good news of blessings and Paradise

51. **Naẓīr** The one who calls man to virtue with warnings of Allah's wrath

52. **Munzir** The one who warns and dissuades from sin

53. **Nūr** The sacred light

54. **Sirāj** The torch of the right path

The one illuminated with the light of faith and Islam.

55. **Miṣbāḥ** The lamp which contains the light of faith and

Islam which lights the realms of worship, submission, and salvation.

56. **Hudā** The guidance to Truth and Paradise

57. **Mahdī** The rightly guided one, guide to the path of knowledge, obedience, and worship

58. **Munīr** The illuminator of the universe

59. **Dā'ī** The one who calls to faith and Islam

60. **Mad'ū** The one who heard and accepted the divine call

61. **Mujīb** The one who accepts prayers

He brought man Allah's ordinances and warned them against sins. He became an example of acting in accordance with His teaching, and he interceded for the good and the sinner alike.

62. **Mujāb** The answered one, the answer to our prayers

63. **Hafī** The true answerer of all questions

64. **'Afū** The clement

He is the example of forgiving the wrong done to him; Allah forgives the one who forgives.

65. **Walī** The friend, of Allah and of all who believe

66. **Ḥaqq** The Truth

67. **Qawī** The powerful

68. **Amīn** The trustworthy

He was called *Muḥammad al-amīn* "Muhammad the trustworthy"—by the Meccans, before he received the divine order to declare his prophethood at the age of 40.

69. **Ma'mūn** The one in whom man confides

70. **Karîm** The generous one

Allah bestows upon him the attribute of one of his beautiful names, the All-Generous One.

71. **Mukarram** The ennobled one

72. **Makîn** The authoritative one

73. **Matîn** The firm and consistent one

74. **Mubîn** The distinguisher and the explainer

75. **Mu'ammil** The hopeful one

76. **Wasūl** The uniter

77. **Dhū quwwah** The source of strength

78. **Dhū ḥurmah** The source of sacredness

79. **Dhū makānah** The source of integrity

80. **Dhū 'izz** The source of might

81. **Dhu faḍl** The source of virtue

82. **Mutā'** The one whom the believers obey

83. **Mutî'** The one who is obedient to Allah

84. **Qidam aṣ-ṣidq** The one constantly sincere

85. **Rahmah** Compassion

86. **Bushrā** Good news

87. **Ghawth** Savior

88. **Ghayth** The beneficent who, like rain which gives life to earth, brings dead hearts to life.

89. **Ghiyāth** The helper

90. **Ni'matullāh** The blessing of Allah

91. **Hadiyatullāh** The gift of Allah to the universe

92. **'Urwah wuthqā** The firm tie that binds man to his Creator

93. **Ṣirāṭullāh** The path leading to Allah and the Truth

94. **Ṣirāṭ mustaqīm** The straight and shortest way leading to Allah

95. **Dhikrullāh** The remembrance of Allah

96. **Sayfullāh** The sword of Allah

97. **Ḥizbullāh** Allah's partisan, destroyer of the enemies of Allah.

98. **Al-najm al-thaqib** The Star whose fire burns devils

99. **Mustafā** The divinely elected

100. **Mujtabā** The chosen one

101. **Muntaqā** The one chosen for his purity

102. **Ummī** The unlettered one who has no teacher among men, who is divinely taught.

103. **Mukhtār** The chosen one who is autonomous

104. **Ajīr** The reward of the believers

105. **Jabbār** The all-compelling one

106. **Abūl-Qāsim** The father of Qasim

107. **Abūl-Ṭāhir** The father of Tahir

108. **Abūl-Ṭayyib** The father of Tayyib

109. **Abū Ibrāhīm** The father of Ibrahim

110. **Mushaffa'** The one given the right of intercession

111. **Shafī'** The intercessor

112. **Sāliḥ** The righteous

113. **Muṣliḥ** The conciliator

114. **Muhaymin** The protector and guardian

115. **Ṣādiq** The truthful

116. **Muṣaddaq** The one proved true by the Truth that comes through him

117. **Sidq** The essence of truthfulness

118. **Sayyid al-mursalīn** The master and best of all Messengers

119. **Imām al-muttaqīn** The leader of the pious who fear Allah

120. **Qā'id al-ghurri al-muhajjalīn** Protector and guide of the believers

121. **Khalīl al-Raḥmān** The close friend of the All-Merciful Allah

122. **Barr** The good and beneficent one

123. **Mabārr** The essence of piety and beneficence

124. **Wajīh** The one distinguished from all else

125. **Naṣīḥ** The true counsellor

126. **Nāṣiḥ** Transformer of men's souls

127. **Wakīl** The faithful trustee

128. **Mutawakkil** The one who puts all his trust in Allah

129. **Kafīl** The guarantor

130. **Shafīq** The compassionate, kind, and benevolent one

131. **Muqim as-sunnah** The one who holds the ordinances of Allah

132. **Muqaddas** The sanctified one

133. **Rūḥ al-quddūs** Essence of the divine

134. **Rūḥ al-ḥaqq** The essence of truth

135. **Rūḥ al-qisṭ** The essence of justice

136. **Kāfī** The one who suffices for the believers

137. **Muktafī** The one sufficient unto himself

138. **Bāligh** The one who has arrived at spiritual perfection

139. **Muballigh** The bearer of news

140. **Shāfī** The curer of sick hearts

141. **Wāṣil** The one who has attained the divine

142. **Mawṣūl** The one who has been attained

143. **Sābiq** The one who precedes everything

144. **Sā'iq** The impelling motive for the faith of the faithful

145. **Hādī** The guide

146. **Muhdī** The one who gives guidance

147. **Muqaddam** The premise of Islam

148. **'Azīz** The highly esteemed beloved has no equal among men

149. **Fāḍil** The one superior in virtue and generosity

150. **Mufaḍḍal** The favored of Allah has been made superior to all beings

151. **Fātiḥ** The conqueror of hearts opens them to faith and truth

152. **Miftāḥ** The key opens the doors of Paradise and locks the doors of Hell

153. **Miftāḥ ar-raḥmah** The key to Allah's mercy

154. **Miftāḥ al-jannah** The key of Paradise

155. **'Alam al-imān** The symbol of faith that leads one to faith

156. 'Alam al-yaqīn The symbol of certitude that leads one to certitude

157. **Dalīl al-khayrāt** The guide to good deeds

158. **Muṣaḥḥiḥ al-ḥasanāt** the one who renders the wrong, right and the not beautiful, beautiful

159. **Muqīl al-atharāt** The foreseer and warner of errors

160. **Ṣafūḥ'an az-ẓallāt** The one who deters errors

161. **Ṣāḥib ash-shafā'ah** The one endowed with intercession

162. **Ṣāḥib al-makān** The one embued with the highest degree of morals and character

163. **Ṣāḥib al qidam** The one endued with the highest station

164. **Makhṣūṣ bil-ʿizz** The one to whom all might and honor are proper

165. **Makhṣūṣ bil-majd** The one to whom all that is noble, sublime, and majestic is proper

166. **Makhṣūṣ bish-sharaf** The one to whom all excellence is proper

167. **Ṣāḥib al-waṣīlah** The possessor of the means to Allah's mercy

168. **Ṣāḥib al-sayf** The owner of the sword against Allah's enemies

169. **Ṣāḥib al-faḍīlah** The source of Allah's grace

170. **Ṣāḥib al-izār** The owner of the cloak of prophet-hood who is mentioned by this name in holy books

171. **Ṣāḥib al-ḥujjah** The possessor of the proof

172. **Ṣāḥib as-sulṭān** The owner of the sovereignty of kings

173. **Ṣāḥib al-ridāʿ** The owner of the woolen cloak

174. **Ṣāḥib ad-darajāt ar-rafiʿah** The one endowed with the exalted station

175. **Ṣāḥib at-taj** The crowned one, crowned with the crown of Paradise on the night of his Ascension

176. **Ṣāḥib al-mighfar** The one who wears the helmet of the holy knight

177. **Ṣāḥib al-liwā'** Holder of the Banner of Praise under which all prophets and believers will gather on the Day of

Last Judgment

178. **Ṣāḥib al-mi'rāj** The master of ascension who was brought, during his lifetime, above the seven heavens, to the divine realms close to Allah

179. **Ṣāḥib al-qaḍīb** The holder of the rod with which he broke the 360 idols around the Kaaba on the day of the conquest of Mecca

180. **Ṣāḥib al-Burāq** The rider of Buraq, the heavenly carrier which brought him from the city of Mecca to Jerusalem on the night of the Ascension

181. **Ṣāḥib al-khātam** The carrier of the Seal of Prophethood, which was between his shoulder blades

182. **Ṣāḥib al-'alāmah** The one endowed with the distinct signs of prophethood

183. **Ṣāḥib al-burhān** The one endowed with the miracles proving his prophethood

184. **Ṣāḥib al-bayan** The one endowed with the greatest expression of prophethood, which is the Holy Qur'an

185. **Faṣīḥ al-lisān** The one whose speech is rendered moṣt eloquent and effective

186. **Muṭahhir al-janān** The source of knowledge, wisdom, and gentleness, whose heart is purified and who purifies hearts

187. **Ra'ūf** The clement one on whom Allah has bestowed His own Name, by which he is mentioned in the Qur'an

188. **Raḥīm** The merciful one, upon whom Allah the Most Merciful bestowed His own Name

189. **Udhn khayr** The hearer of good

190. **Ṣaḥīḥ al-Islām** The truth of Islam which corrects and cancels man's distortions of divine truths previously revealed and reestablishes the true message of Allah

191. **Sayyid al-kawnayn** The master of all created beings in this world and the Hereafter

192. **'Ayn al-na'īm** The source through which Allah's blessings come in this world and the Hereafter

193. **'Ayn al-qurr** The source of light and splendor

194. **Sa'd Allāh** The joy of Allah who as the first created intelligence, contains the salvation, the victory, peace, and blessing, of all creation

195. **Sa'd al-khalq** The joy of all created beings, being the best and the most generous and closest to Allah among them

196. **Khaṭīb al-umām** The preacher to humanity

197. **'Alam al-hudā** The sign of guidance to truth, Allah's pleasure, and Paradise

198. **Kāshif al-karb** The one who lifts the pain, afflictions, and difficulties from man

199. **Rāfi' al-rutab** The one who raises the levels of those who believe and obey him

200. **'Izz al-r'āb** The glory of the Arabs

201. **Ṣāḥib al-faraj** The source of consolation, who gives bliss and comfort to those who believe in his prophethood and follow his commands.

BISMILLĀH AR-RAḤMĀN AR-RAḤĪM

O Allah, we pray that You bestow Your mercy, grace, and blessings upon our Master Muhammad so that by this prayer You will deliver us from all fears and from our lowliness; that You will cleanse us of all our impurities, and that You will send to us the ultimate of all good in this life and in the Hereafter.

O most loving Allah, the Benefactor of all things. O Unique Creator of the heavens and the earth. O Living, Self-Sufficient Allah. O Master of all greatness, majesty and graciousness—In the name of Your exalted Essence, we beg that You change our nature from the nature of man and that You raise our station to that of the most elevated of Your angels. O Transformer and Keeper of our condition and our power, transform our state into the best of states. Glorified and praised be You, O Allah. I bear witness that there is no god besides You: from You do I seek forgiveness, and unto You do I turn repentant. O Allah, bestow Your blessings and grace upon our Master Muhammad and upon his Family and Companions.